THE CHRISTIAN WARFARE AND ARMOUR

THE
CHRISTIAN WARFARE
AND ARMOUR

James Philip

VICTORY PRESS

EASTBOURNE

© JAMES PHILIP 1972

ISBN 0 85476 173 X

These studies were originally given
at Holyrood Abbey Church, Edinburgh,
and the spoken form has been largely
retained.

Printed in Great Britain for
VICTORY PRESS (Evangelical Publishers Ltd)
Lottbridge Drove, Eastbourne, Sussex
by Richard Clay (The Chaucer Press) Ltd,
Bungay, Suffolk

Contents

'Finally, my brethren, be strong in the Lord,
and in the power of his might.
Put on the whole armour of God, that ye may
be able to stand against the wiles of the
devil.
For we wrestle not against flesh and blood,
but against principalities, against powers,
against the rulers of the darkness of this
world, against spiritual wickedness in high
places.
Wherefore take unto you the whole armour of
God, that ye may be able to withstand in the
evil day, and having done all, to stand.
Stand therefore, with your loins girt about
with truth, and having on the breastplate
of righteousness;
And your feet shod with the preparation of
the gospel of peace;
Above all, taking the shield of faith, wherewith
ye shall be able to quench all the fiery darts
of the wicked.
And take the helmet of salvation, and the
sword of the Spirit, which is the word of God:
Praying always with all prayer and supplication
in the Spirit, and watching thereunto with
all perseverance and supplication for all
saints;
And for me, that utterance may be given unto
me, that I may open my mouth boldly, to make
known the mystery of the gospel,
For which I am an ambassador in bonds; that
therein I may speak boldly, as I ought to
speak.'

Ephesians 6. 10–20

I

INTRODUCTORY

WE ARE setting out to consider what has been termed the Christian armour as Paul describes it in the impressive closing passage of the Epistle to the Ephesians.

Let me say first of all by way of introduction that the teaching of this passage became very real and came to mean a great deal to me when I was passing through a time of fierce and prolonged testing, when all the powers of darkness seemed to be let loose on my soul and were intent, so it seemed, on bringing me crashing down; and it was in those days that God revealed to me two things: the richness and completeness of our position in Christ and what He has made us in Him, and the divine provision in the armour of light against all the assaults of the enemy. In those days morning prayer was for me a matter of poring over this passage in urgent desperation, seeking to put on this divine armour piece by piece, to preserve me against the assaults of the devil that were sure to come before the day was very far advanced; some of the things that I shall be saying about this passage—and I hope I have learned more about it over the years since then—come from the fires of very real and bitter experience and from a very desperately real situation as well as from the objective and, I hope, faithful exposition of the Word of God.

These two things that I have mentioned which became so real to me in those days—what we are and have in Christ, and the divine provision in the armour of God—are in fact very closely linked in the Epistle to the Ephesians.

Paul begins the Epistle with a statement of the believer's wealth in Christ. The believer is blessed with all spiritual blessings in heavenly places in Christ. A believer is one who has received those blessings from the God and Father of our Lord Jesus Christ. And the apostle instances some of these blessings that are ours, what we have in Christ: redemption through His blood, adoption, inheritance, and so on. Then in the second half of chapter 1 he proceeds to pray that believers may know just how rich is their condition, that they may know the exceeding greatness of God's power to usward who believe, and then he proceeds to explain and define that power in terms of Christ's victory in His death and resurrection, by which He is raised far above all principality and power and made head over all things to the church. The connection, then, between these statements in chapter 1 and this passage in chapter 6 is surely plain. In chapter 1 we read of the blessings in heavenly places that are bestowed on believers, and that aspect of these blessings that has to do specifically with the bestowal of power, and all linked and associated with the victory of the lordship of Christ—then here, in chapter 6, verse 10, we read of the sphere of the warfare of the Christian in the heavenly places, the enemy to be faced, the principalities and powers over whom Christ has been raised and exalted for us. It is the same thought forms, in both cases. Look again at chapter 1, verse 19. First the prayer that we may know what is the exceeding greatness of His power to usward who believe, according to the working of His mighty power which He wrought in Christ when He raised Him from the dead and set Him at His own right hand in heavenly places. Then, in chapter 6, the wrestling in heavenly places ('high places' in chapter 6 is exactly the same in the Greek as 'heavenly places' in chapter 1), far above all principality and power and might and dominion and every name that is named, not only in this world but also in that which is to come. Principality, power, might, dominion—these are what we are wrestling against, says Paul; against principalities, against powers, against the rulers of the darkness of this world, against spiritual wickedness in heavenly places. And God has put all things under His feet (1, 22), and gave Christ to be head over all things to the church; all these things, all these powers.

And then Paul says, 'Be strong in the Lord.' That is to say, what he gives us here (6. 10) is an exhortation based (i) on the statement of fact that he gives in chapter 1 and (ii) on the prayer that he has made for believers. In other words Paul is making a two-fold statement: about Christ's warfare and victory, and about our warfare and victory, and the one based on the other. Now it is important that we see this, to get the context of Paul's teaching here about the Christian warfare and the Christian armour. To put it another way, the believer must lay hold of, and enter into, the victory that has been won for him by Christ. And the personal appropriation by faith of that victory is certainly no sinecure or automatic thing but something that exercises the believer to the very fullest extent. It is the fight of faith, it is a battle, a warfare, and sometimes a fight to the bitter end. Here, then, is the first lesson that we gather : we do not go to this warfare, the warfare of the Christian life, on our own charges; we battle from a position of victory that has been given us, and it is a question of appropriating what is ours in the gift of God, and making it our own. This is the point in the hymn :

> Take, my soul, thy full salvation.
> Rise o'er sin and fear and care.
> Think what Spirit dwells within you.

Now you see, this is a conscious effort of faith— 'Take my soul, thy full salvation.' It is not automatically ours. We are to lay hold upon eternal life, and as a matter of daily spiritual exercise we are to 'think what Spirit dwells within us'. This is the point of having 'quiet times', as we call them. A quiet time is not a time for an automatic reading of a part of Scripture and saying a few prayers. A quiet time in one sense is a very busy time, it is very unquiet, and ought to be unquiet. If we are battling—and a great part of the Christian life consists of battling—it is simply a question of day by day thinking who we are and what we are, telling ourselves what we are in

Christ. You know how in the first waking moments of a new day there is that wonderful sense of euphoria before the thoughts of what lies before us sweep in upon us; and then we say, 'Oh dear, another day!', and we just want to escape back into the oblivion of sleep again. But in that first moment when we feel so good, before we begin to feel that we cannot face that day—it is then that the thinking has to come in. We say, 'I can't face this day', but God says, 'My child, you can, you must, and you will. Think what Spirit dwells within you.' So that over the circumstances of the day—this is how practical it is—over against the circumstances of the day, and your sense of weakness and inability to face it, you must think of what God has done. Yes, you are going to face terrible trials this day, but think 'what a Father's smile is thine.' You are facing them with the smile of God upon you. Now this is bound to do something to us. And this is Paul's point. We are to appropriate, be strong in the Lord, so that right at the outset of our day before the battles ever begin, or the enemy marshals his forces, we are to gird on our armour, be strong in the Lord, by thinking what we are or have in Christ, appropriating and making our own what God has given us in Him. Hence the three imperatives, Be strong, Put on the armour of God, Take unto you the armour of God. This is the pattern. What a practical thing it is! And the more desperate our situation, the more practical we will find these mighty words to be for us day by day.

Next, the nature of the conflict that Paul describes here. It is, as he says, with principalities and powers.

I do not intend spending time now establishing the reality of dark powers, demonic powers at work in human life. Let it suffice to say here just a word about the variety of approach made by these powers. The fact that they are instanced separately, each with the word 'against'—against flesh and blood, against principalities, against powers, against the rulers of the darkness of this world, against spiritual wickedness in high places—suggests, as one commentator has put it, that these various powers have different functions. And it is certainly true, from the Scriptures we see this to be true, that there are different approaches to the souls of men. There is the approach along the line of temptation to sin for example, but there are other approaches also that the evil one makes. There are the attacks upon health that he makes on God's servants. That is different from temptation to sin; it is not a question of sin as such that is involved there, but a destroying attack. There are the attempts to hinder. You remember how on more than one occasion Paul says in his letters that he wanted to go to a particular place, but Satan hindered him. What does that mean? It does not refer to temptation to sin; it refers to obstructions unaccountably being put in the way; and Paul says this is the work of Satan. An enemy has done this. Then there are these strange and dark experiences through which believers sometimes pass, in which they seem to be being accused by Satan before God, with pointing fingers robbing them of their peace. Now that is nothing to do with temptation to sin, but something separate. Then there are the attacks from Satan which are designed to frustrate the believer, and those which are designed to oppress him. I remember many years ago, before I ever met Dr. Irvine of Ekwendeni, getting a circular letter that had come from his pen, in which he described an experience through which he had passed when strange pressures were bearing down upon his spirit, bringing a darkness upon him. He had never experienced such a thing before. He really thought he was going off his head, until he recognised that this was an attack of the enemy. You see, this is the function of the principalities, of the powers, the rulers of the darkness of this world, the spiritual wickednesses—different approaches. And Paul says, 'Know your enemy.'

Now it would be a study in itself to go into all these different modes of attack; they are all so terribly real at times devastating. But for the present we simply assume their reality, and also the fact that we recognise them for what they are. The point of our study is to be how to combat them and to resist them when they come. Let it suffice to say that recognition of them is of course absolutely vital. You do not fight an enemy if you do not know he is there, and not knowing he is there gives him a free hand. It is always a good and necessary exercise to examine the Scriptures and their references to Satan's various wiles, his voice and his guises. His voice, for example, is heard only three times in the whole of the Scriptures—in the garden of Eden, in the story of Job, and at the temptation of Jesus Christ. Surely there is something there for us to learn! And nobody who takes the reality of Satan seriously can afford not to examine these three places in the Scriptures and examine them very carefully, where his voice is heard (his influence, of course, is everywhere).

One other thing in this introductory word. It is no sign, when we are under attack, that we are failing as Christians. Being terribly troubled, for example, by temptation does not mean that we are not living the Christian life properly. Indeed, in this context, it may mean the exact opposite, for it is precisely when we are what we should be that Satan turns his malevolent attention upon us most acutely. As an old Puritan once said, 'He that standeth near his captain is a sure target for the archers.' Indeed, in terms of Paul's teaching in the earlier part of the Epistle to the Ephesians, it is when we enter experimentally into our position in Christ, that is to say, into the heavenly places (cf. Ephesians 2. 6—He has raised us up together with Christ and made us sit together with Christ in heavenly places), when we take our full salvation and enter into the thrill and enjoyment and glory of it, that we most of all draw the attentions of the enemy, for the heavenly places are the sphere in which he operates. He is the prince of the power of the air, after all, that is his realm. And it is not by accident that one of the themes which leads up to and into this exposition of the Christian warfare is a statement about being filled with the Holy Spirit. To be filled with the Holy Spirit is not the answer to the problems of the believer in that sense, but the signal for problems and attacks really to begin in earnest.

Now to the armour itself. I want to say some

general things about it before embarking on a detailed examination of each component part, and I want to make three observations in particular.

(i) Some commentators have suggested that Paul is using the analogy of the Roman soldier's armour here, in the picture that he gives. And certainly Paul had much experience of Roman soldiers—at the time he wrote these words he was being guarded by them in the prison in Rome—and it is not difficult to imagine him looking up from his writing materials to the guard standing by him and, as it were, noting down the various parts of the armour. But all the same it is probably more likely, knowing Paul, that he had in mind some other consideration, namely, the Old Testament picture of the divine warrior in the Book of the prophet Isaiah. See Isaiah 59. 14 and the following verses. Isaiah is depicting a time of great crisis and great difficulty for the life of the people. 'Judgment is turned away backward, and justice standeth afar off: for truth is fallen in the street, and equity cannot enter. Yea, truth faileth; and he that departeth from evil maketh himself a prey: and the Lord saw it, and it displeased him that there was no judgment. And he saw that there was no man, and wondered that there was no intercessor: therefore his arm brought salvation unto him; and his righteousness, it sustained him. For he put on righteousness as a breastplate, and an helmet of salvation upon his head, and he put on the garments of vengeance for clothing, and was clad with zeal as a cloke. According to their deeds, accordingly he will repay, fury to his adversaries, recompense to his enemies; to

the islands he will repay recompense. So shall they
fear the name of the Lord from the west, and his
glory from the rising of the sun. When the enemy
shall come in like a flood, the Spirit of the Lord shall
lift up a standard against him.' Now, as I say, knowing Paul, it is much more likely that he drew his
illustration from the Scriptures than from the
Roman soldiers round about him. For the significance
of this quotation in Isaiah, if that is what Paul had in
mind, is that Paul is taking words, and applying them
to the Christian and the Christian armour, that were
first spoken of God and of the divine Messiah, the
divinely appointed King. Now this is the wonderful
thing. He takes the armour that God wore, in this
vision in Isaiah 59, to execute His victory over his
enemies, and he applies that armour to the believer in
Christ. So that the armour of God, as Paul puts it
here in Ephesians 6, is not only the armour which
God supplies to his children; it is also His own
armour, given to us for the same fight as He was involved in. This is the link, once again, between our
thought earlier on of Christ's victory in chapter 1
and our victory in chapter 6. Do you not think it is
wonderful that the armour with which Christ was
clad for His battle against His foes is the armour that
is made available to us for our battle, and for our
victory? It is one and the same battle, you see. We
are entering into and appropriating what He has
done for us, but to do this we need His armour.
Wherefore take unto you the whole armour of God.
As the master so the servant, and as the armour so
also the victory. That is a great encouragement to us.

We are clad in the armour in which Christ was clad.

(ii) In the second place it may well be, as I have already suggested, that the various parts of the armour are meant to be taken as safeguards against various different kinds of attack from the enemy. Think, for example, of the satanic attack against Adam and Eve in the Garden of Eden which expressed itself as the sowing of doubt in Eve's mind about the word of God. What did Satan say? 'Yea, hath God said, ye shall not eat of every tree of the garden?' And a seed of doubt was planted in Eve's heart, as she began to doubt God's word. Now in a situation like that one sees the force of putting on the girdle of truth. Have your loins girt about with truth, to safeguard you against the lies of the devil. Or, for example, think of the attacks that Satan sometimes makes on men's minds. I instanced Dr. Kenneth Irvine years ago, and the pressures upon his mind. He really thought he was going to go mad. Well, if Satan is attacking your mind, you need the helmet of salvation, because the helmet is to guard your head. This is the kind of way that we must think of this armour without being needlessly meticulous or splitting hairs. We must recognise that these are all legitimate insights into the question.

(iii) The third thing is this. Commentators have sometimes seen a progression in the warfare in which we are involved, as exemplified in these verses. Those who have read the Rev. W. Still's book, *Toward Spiritual Maturity* will recall that he has expressed this idea very well indeed when he speaks of a three-fold progression: Strategic retreat ('Be strong in the Lord'), Unyielding defence (the defensive parts of the armour), and then All-out attack ('the sword of the Spirit which is the word of God'). Well then, let us think of this for a little time. First of all Christ is a shelter to hide in. Secondly, He is a position to stand in, and thirdly He is a base to attack from. Now although we speak of a progression there, it might perhaps be better thought of as a development, for each one of these is dependent on the other. For example, our shelter is always in the Lord, and there is a sense in which we never venture out of that shelter, and we cannot dare to venture out of it. Then our stand is always on His finished work, and we dare not move from that stand for a moment, and on the wealth of our position in Him. And it is from these two points that we go forward to attack the enemy. Depending on the aspect of the warfare, what we need may be first of all the consciousness of the divine shelter. I have mentioned the experience of waking up in the morning and being conscious of all that is going to face us that day rushing in upon us, and we feel we just cannot face it; we want to run away. Well, if you want to run away, run into Christ. Be strong in the Lord. Get into your fortress. 'What time my heart is overwhelmed, lead me to the rock,' says the Psalmist, 'that is higher than I; for Thou has been a shelter for me, and a strong tower from the enemy.' Now it does not matter how weak you are if you are inside that tower. 'The name of the Lord is a strong tower: the righteous runneth into it and is safe.' How many a soul has found protection and deliverance in whispering the name of the Lord in their hour of need! The Lord is our rock, a shelter in the time of storm. Now this is one of the things Paul means when he says, 'Be strong in the Lord.' You have no strength in yourself, but in the Lord is everlasting strength, so that we have a shelter to hide in.

From another point of view, we are under attack and we stand firm. Stand! This word keeps coming up in the passage. Stand, stand, stand, in unyielding defence, clad in heavenly armour, with our loins girt with truth, breastplate of righteousness, feet shod with the preparation of the gospel, shield of faith, helmet of salvation. These defensive weapons help us to stand, and enable us to stand, against all the wiles of the devil; unyielding defence, overshadowed with the panoply of God. Thanks be to God who giveth us the victory! It is His victory, and He gives us this victory to use against the enemy, because it was won for us. Now, you see, to realise this, and to think this, and to be conscious of it and make it our own, means that we will stand. We have nothing to keep us from standing.

And then, the attack. And perhaps this is a point we least remember about in the Christian warfare. The best form of defence is attack, all the military strategists insist, and how true it is in the spiritual life! The enemy is to be attacked! We carry the war into his camp, and there is nothing that demoralises Satan so much as a believer gritting his teeth and saying, 'I'll get even with you for this, you devil', and fighting and attacking. C. S. Lewis so usefully points out that this is what hatred is for. Hatred of humans is always wrong, but hatred of evil and hatred of the enemy—this is how we can vent our spleen, that is what a spleen is for; it is the only legitimate expression of it, getting our own back on the devil through the sword of the Spirit which is the Word of God. Of course this is something that Satan tries to prevent, and he whispers in the hearts of believers, 'You? You cannot witness for Christ; you are a flop, you are a failure, there is not much point in you preaching, is there?' But he knows that if once that believer who has stumbled and fallen gets up again, and starts wielding the sword of the Spirit, he will be the one to suffer. Take the sword of the Spirit which is the Word of God, praying always—the weapon of all-prayer, you see. A shelter to hide in, a position to stand on, a base to attack from; that is the Christian warfare, and we shall begin to look at the individual aspects of it in the next chapter, and turn to the girdle of truth about the loins, why it should come first and foremost, what it means, how we can put it on, and what it can do for us in the battle of the Lord.

2

THE GIRDLE OF TRUTH

WE TURN now to a consideration of the first part of the armour, the girdle of truth. 'Stand, therefore, having girded your loins with truth' (the verb is active, 'having girded'). The idea of girding the loins is of course a familiar one in the Scriptures, and its meaning can hardly be in doubt in general terms. You may recall an interesting reference in the Book of Daniel chapter 5, in the story of Belshazzar. We are told how when the writing appeared on the wall it so unnerved the King that—this is how the description reads—'the king's countenance was changed, and his thoughts troubled him, so that the joints of his loins were loosed, and his knees smote one against another'. That expresses the opposite of what Paul in the spiritual sense is advocating here. The king was demoralised, he was ungirt. And for a soldier to have his loins girt means therefore that he has pulled himself together both bodily and mentally, and put on the girdle which holds together the garments so as to enable work to be done and battle to be fought. Now the girdle is mentioned first of all because it keeps the other parts in place. This is strategic in the spiritual sense—and indeed the truth is strategic in the spiritual sense, whatever meaning we place upon that phrase. You will remember how Peter in his Epistle calls on his people to gird up the loins of their mind. This is exactly the same idea as here; and Jesus said, 'Let your loins be girded about and your light burning', an echo perhaps from the passover story in Exodus where the people of God were told to eat the passover with loins girt and staff in hand, that is, ready to move out. A general state of readiness, therefore, is indicated here.

Now how can we be at the ready when the devil attacks us? The girdle which is to provide this state of readiness and preparedness is—truth. How are we to understand this word? Well, some think of it in terms of truth of doctrine, and others think of it in terms of truth of heart, that is to say, sincerity or integrity. Now it is not at all clear to me that these differing interpretations must necessarily be alternatives, as if it must be either the one or the other. Why not both? In fact both have relevance in this connection, and it seems to me that the one flows from the other. It is questionable whether from a biblical point of view either of the two could ever have been thought of in isolation from the other. I do not think the biblical writers made this kind of distinction when they thought of truth; both things would necessarily be in their minds, and quite frankly even if that were not so, from the practical, spiritual point of view we as Christians dare not exclude either the one or the other from our thinking, lest by doing so we deprive ourselves of any divine protection in the battle. This is the practical consideration. It is not an academic question, and we are not going to argue the point now whether in fact Paul meant gospel truth, the truth of the Word of God on the one hand, or truth in terms of sincerity of heart, as if these were mutually exclusive alternatives We shall take them both, and be sure and be safe. And so we look at each in turn.

First of all, truth of doctrine. To have on the girdle of truth—in the sense of having this holding all else in place, that is, having the girdle of truth as the integral and foundational part of all the armour, which alone keeps the soldier from being disorganised and put into disarray—means, quite simply, to allow the truth of God to be a living reality in our lives, to live by it, to act upon it, to breath it, to let it govern our conduct and our attitude day by day, as a second nature. To be steeped in the truth of God, to be garrisoned by the truth of God—this is what Paul means. He speaks in Colossians 3, for example, of letting the word of Christ dwell in us richly in all wisdom; that is the idea. Now there are a number of Scripture references which convey this particular insight. In Psalm 119. 11 we have the words, 'Thy word have I hid in mine heart, that I might not sin against thee.' That is the girdle of truth. In John 17. 17, in the great prayer of our Lord in the Upper Room, 'Sanctify them through thy truth : thy word is truth.' That is the girdle of truth. And in James' Epistle 1. 19, 21 'Be swift to hear . . . and receive with meekness the engrafted word, which is able to save your souls'— in the hour of temptation or at any other time. That is the girdle of truth. It was said of Martin Luther that he was a man whose conscience was captive to the Word of God, that is to say, his conscience was gripped and in the control of the Word of God. This is the meaning that we are to put upon this phrase in the first instance. Let us ask ourselves: Are our lives under control of the Word of God today? If they are they are under protection from all the works of the enemy. We sometimes speak of a man as being a man of the Word, and we mean by that that his life is so thoroughly steeped in the Scriptures that everything he does, everything he says, everything he thinks is conditioned and controlled and dictated by the Word of God. He is a man who, like the Psalmist, not only meditates on God's law, but delights in it. 'O how I love thy law,' he cries: 'it is my meditation day and night.' Now such a man is one who is safeguarded and fortified for the battle. He will be kept. This is the practical exhortation that we are given in this word today. Let our lives be steeped in the Holy Scriptures. Let the Scriptures master our very inmost being, and our loins will be girt about with truth.

But this must be insisted: it is no mere use of Scripture as a charm. It is knowledge and belief of the truth, truth spiritually apprehended and believed, as to its significance and import, and yielded to. As one commentator puts it, 'To enter on this spiritual conflict ignorant or doubting would be to enter battle blind and lame' (Hodge). Now this is what I mean by being gripped by the truth, mastered by it, fired by it. When a man is fired by the truth of God he is invincible. That is why Paul prays so earnestly in the first chapter of the Epistle, 'that ye may know

... what is the exceeding greatness of his power to usward who believe.' You could almost put it like this: 'that you may experience as a practical reality in your lives the exceeding greatness of the power that is to usward.'

Let me illustrate. You will remember how Paul, during the testing time of the storm at sea, when he was being taken from Palestine to Rome for his trial —a storm, we may say, that was certainly no ordinary storm but was engineered specifically by Satan with a view to destroying this man who had done such harm to his kingdom of darkness—received an assurance from God that all would be well with him and that none would be lost from the ship's company. And his reaction was this: 'Wherefore, sirs, be of good cheer: for I believe God, that it shall be even as it was told me.' 'I believe God.' You see? He was girt about with the truth of God, the truth of the promise, not merely in the sense of taking the promise to heart, but also girding himself with the knowledge of all that that promising God was, in His Person and His character. He believed God, he committed himself to the word of God. This was the truth of God and it was the God of truth who had promised him and assured him, and he girt himself about with it. And nobody can read that story without being conscious of this man standing calm and serene in the midst of the panic and the fear and the dread all around him. He stands like a colossus among pygmies. He is girt about with the truth of God. And so also, often in our own personal assurance, we make our response to it, and we hang on to that word, and in the midst of the battle we say, 'Lord, Thou saidst . . .' You see what we are doing? We are girding our loins with truth. 'Lord, Thou saidst'—'You said you would do this, Lord, I'm looking to you.'

Or, to take another illustration, to be thoroughly practical and specific: suppose in our reading one morning we come, let us say, to the famous chapter, 1 Corinthians 13, on love. 'Love suffereth long, and is kind; love envieth not, love thinketh no evil', and so on. Well now, we take this word, we meditate upon it, we seek to allow our hearts to be mastered by it. And then, it may be during the day a careless word is spoken in company in our hearing, and we take it to ourselves, and we imagine some nasty spirit behind it, thinking it was a deliberate attempt to slight us or belittle us, when all the time it was simply an unfortunate turn of expression with no ill intent (this is so often how misunderstandings of this nature arise). Well, if I allow myself to brood over that, and let it affect my whole demeanour, let it colour my whole day, then I have forgotten the word that I read in the morning which said, 'Love thinketh no evil.' I am thinking evil, I am putting the worst construction on what I heard. There was no offence meant or intended, but my loins are ungirt, and the devil has got in and he has ruined my day. You see? This is how practical it is. Now to have one's loins girt about with truth is to be impregnable in a situation like that, and that is very practical is it not? Have you never had that experience? Have you never misconstrued what somebody said in your hearing? You took it as an affront and an insult but it was never meant like that. But you brooded over it and it poisoned your whole soul. You know, people have been known to leave a church for a thing like that. Have your loins girt about with truth!

But we can go further. The truth of God, the truth of the gospel, and hearts and lives gripped and mastered in that way are hearts and lives that are invincible, and impregnable by the attacks of the enemy. But we could be more specific still in relation to the truth of God. There is what I could call, for want of a better name 'battle truth'. There is such a thing as battle truth in the New Testament, that body of truth that is so essential for mature Christian experience and given by Paul, for example, in the Epistle to the Romans. I have often thought that no one is likely ever to wage a good warfare, or be a good soldier of Jesus Christ, who has not made it his business to grasp the teachings of this mighty Epistle and be grasped and mastered by it. You remember how Paul takes eleven whole chapters to unfold the magnificent and majestic truths of salvation and redemption before ever he comes to the point where he says, 'I beseech you therefore, brethren, by the mercies of God, that you present your bodies a living sacrifice, holy, acceptable unto God, which is your reasonable service'—eleven chapters to expound the gospel of grace before he exhorts us to respond to it, teaching us about the lost and guilty state of mankind, his inability to recover righteousness: Christ set forth as a propitiation; justification by faith; identification with Christ in death and resurrection;

the liberty of the believer in and through the Spirit—
then, Present your bodies. To live much in that at-
mosphere will mean to be girt about with truth; and
that is what Paul advocates in this wonderful word.
Stand therefore, not in your own strength—that is
the surest way to failure, to immediate failure—but
girt about with truth in that sense.

Now let us look at this from the other standpoint,
truth of heart. Truth of doctrine and truth of heart,
in the sense of sincerity and integrity, it seems to me.
necessarily go together, because the one produces the
other. Perhaps no more systematic presentation of
the truth of God has ever been given than that given
by Calvinism in the Reformed Church. Let me quote
to you a judgment passed on Calvinism by a famous
writer some years ago. This is what he said: 'The
Calvinists attracted to themselves every man in
Europe that hated a lie. . . . They abhorred, as no
body of men ever more abhorred, all conscious men-
dacity, all impurity, all moral wrong of any kind so
far as they could recognise it. Whatever exists at
this moment in England and Scotland of conscien-
tious fear of wrongdoing is the remnant of the convictions which were branded by the Calvinists into
the people's hearts. (J. A. Froude). Well, cause and
effect! Truth of doctrines, truth of heart, the one
producing the other. Look at Paul's epistles. They all
require and expect truth in the inward parts as the
expression of our response to the truth of the gospel;
and no one who is not this—true in this sense—need
hope or expect to win the battle.

Who can fight for truth and God,
Enthralled by lies and sin?
He who would wage such war on earth
Must first be true within.

What is referred to here is inner sincerity, single-mindedness, straightness, these things which are the product of grace in the soul, and without which Christian profession and the Christian life are empty things. Do you remember what God said to Abraham in Genesis 17? 'Walk before me and be thou perfect.' That phrase could very fairly be rendered, 'Walk before me and be thou straight.' You see, the Christian life is no place for insincerity, or sham, or pretence. Everything unreal must be stripped from us. Single-minded sincerity is what is called for. James says, 'A double-minded man is unstable in all his ways.' Truth in the inward parts is what God desires and requires. To be sincere with others—and with oneself—loins girt about with truth in that sense. Now when I say that, I am not saying anything essentially different from 'loins girt about with the truth of God or the truth of the gospel'. The two things belong together. You cannot have your loins girt about with the truth of the gospel without also being this, as an inevitable consequence.

Think of some of the phrases which are used of certain people in describing their general attitude to life and to others. We sometimes speak, for example, of people who 'have their eye on the main chance', and by that we mean a man who is an opportunist in the worst sense of that term. He is the kind of man who will trample on others to gain his objective. He is a man who will show and offer friendship only in so far as it pleases him and in so far as it is advantageous to him to do so, and when that friendship can further his interest no more he casts it off. He is basically an insincere person, and sadly enough there are people like that in the Christian church who make use of others. Now that is the kind of person who is going to fall in battle, in the evil day, because his loins are ungirt. He is basically an untrue person. Then there is the even greater hazard of insincerity with oneself. There are in fact whole areas of our inner being where insincerity can lurk. There is the double mind, as James calls it, the double life, the secret life, the secret indulgences, the dabbling in things that we cannot square with our best conscience and convictions, but do them nevertheless. Are you living a double life? I do not mean anything necessarily gross. But is there a private sector in your life which is kept strictly separate from the spiritual? To have loins girt about with truth means to be true there, in the private sector. Then there are the deeper levels in which unconscious dishonesty may hold sway. I am thinking, for example, of the psychological drive that often animates Christian people and which has to do duty for a true spiritual impetus, and so on. Well might David cry for truth in the inward parts! Now these are the areas where we have got to let God's word search our hearts ruthlessly. We just cannot afford to be untrue there, otherwise we will go down. A man who has a psychological drive in his personality is a man who will not survive the Christian battle. His loins are not girt with truth. Truth is lacking. His life does not square. There are problems to be resolved, I am not necessarily saying the man is culpable, but he is sick, and there are problems to be solved there before he can be really serviceable for God.

I said in chapter 1 that the various parts of the armour may well correspond to different kinds of attacks from the enemy, and we must look now at this possibility in both senses of the word that we have just considered. First of all, there is the attack on our belief of the truth. This is one of Satan's recognised wiles. In the Garden of Eden, this was how the attack came to Adam and Eve. Satan sowed doubts in their hearts about the word of God. 'Yea, hath God said?' And the deed was done. And this is often how Satan does in fact attack people: the sowing of doubts about God's word and its full inspiration, for example. If Satan can establish secret reservations in our hearts and minds about the Bible, although he may not prevent us from serving God he will make sure that we go forward halting and crippled. Listen to these words written by James Denney sixty years ago. 'How many are there whose minds have been secretly loosened from what once seemed convictions, who have been intellectually estranged from the gospel, who would create a sensation if they stood up in the midst of Christian worship and revealed their whole thoughts about God and Christ, about Church and Bible, about Prayer and Sacraments.' Indeed! Doubtless Denney is thinking particularly of ministers of the gospel, and this is certainly true of them,

but it is by no means confined to them. Loins girt
about with truth! Hold fast to the truth of the God-
inspired Scriptures, whatever the cost, even when
your own intelligence seems to have the final answer.
Back the integrity of the Word of God against the
validity of your intelligence every time. Remember
that your intelligence also was tainted by the Fall,
and is a fallen thing. The Word of God is God-
breathed and therefore authoritative. This, then, is
sometimes where Satan comes in. If he can spread
confusion and uncertainty in a man's mind about the
Word of God, about the truth of God, about what to
believe, he has effectively disarmed that soldier. He
will not be able to fight the battles of the Lord. He is
confused, he is ignorant. He is mixed up, and he is a
victim of Satan.

But an attack can come in the other sense of the
word too, an attack on single-minded sincerity. And
it is here that the temptation is sometimes very subtle
to allow a double standard. Hear again the words of
James Denney. 'We sit here side by side in the
Church, but how far are we really present to each
other? How many of us are there who have things to
hide? How many who have done what no one knows
and what they have not told unreservedly even to
God? How many are there whose minds are quietly
and steadily set on something which they dare not
avow, whose future depends on keeping others in the
dark, and who do not realise that . . . the very same
act keeps themselves in the dark too?' Truth, sincerity,
the double standard. I remember what the Rev. John
Macbeth of Inverness once told me some years ago

about an encounter he had with a man who had been greatly used of God in evangelism. It was discovered that the man was living a lie; he was living a double life, and when he was challenged about it he said with a deprecating laugh, 'Oh well, but everybody has a skeleton in the cupboard, haven't they?' And I remember John Macbeth's flashing eyes as he told me, and the look of horror in his face. A double standard? Truth in the inward parts? That is the temptation that Satan brings to us. And he whispers, 'No one will know, anyway. Reserve the right to yourself to have another standard in the secret compartment.' And then we wonder why in the evil day we see some saints just crumpling and going down without a fight. That is why. Their loins are ungirt. The truth has not been put on. Satan has got in with the suggestion of a double standard. How many of us are there who have things to hide? Have you got things to hide today? This is the point at issue. Paul says, 'Stand therefore, having your loins girt about with truth.' Let the truth of the gospel grip you afresh until it grips that secret compartment and squeezes out the insincerity, the living lie, the unhallowed thing, until it makes you true, utterly and completely true. Then you will stand in the evil day and having done all you will be found still standing. God grant that it may be so.

3

THE BREASTPLATE OF RIGHTEOUSNESS

WE TURN now to the second part of the Christian armour. We have just spoken of 'loins girt about with truth'; now it is 'having on, or having put on, the breastplate of righteousness'. I think that in the interpretation of the various parts of the Christian armour it becomes clearer and clearer that they are all linked with one another in reference to the spiritual provision of the gospel. Nevertheless the imagery here is very significant. The breastplate guards the heart which is the vital organ of the body. If the heart can be got at, then the battle is won; and if Satan can get to the heart, then the battle is won for him and lost for us; and this, of course, is what the enemy seeks to do. He tries to get to the very heart of our resistance with arrows of doubt and confusion. If he can make us doubt our salvation, he will not have much trouble with us; we will be paralysed as to effective battle. No one can fight for God if he has doubts about his own salvation. If the trumpet make an uncertain sound who will prepare himself for the battle? One has only to think, for example, what it meant in the 16th century that Martin Luther should have had on the breastplate of righteousness, to realise how all-important it is for victory.

In the last chapter I suggested that we should take truth in the two possible senses which commentators have given—truth in the sense of the word truth, the gospel of truth, and truth in the sense of personal sincerity and straightness—the one following from the other. I cannot understand why commentators should be so emphatic in saying that it means the one and not the other. They say this, but they do not say why they say it; and this is too important a subject for us to miss any possible help we can get out of it; so I want to take righteousness also in the two possible senses in which it can be taken; first of all referring to imputed righteousness—and that opens up the whole matter of the justification of God—and then, as a necessary corollary to that, personal righteousness. The one follows the other and flows from the other.

We shall think first of all, then, of righteousness in the theological or doctrinal sense in which it is portrayed for example in the Epistle to the Romans, the righteousness of God imputed to us. Now I find with Christian people that it is one thing for them to have accepted Christ as Saviour, but quite another thing for them to understand how this puts them in the right with God. What I mean by this is that a man can genuinely accept Christ as his Saviour and still be very confused as to how doing that puts him right in the sight of God. And I find very often that it is those who are hazy and confused about what has happened to them that become easy prey to the wiles of the enemy, and become unsatisfactory in their

Christian experience, and do not grow to maturity. On the other hand, those who are clear and instructed on all these matters tend to stand firm and go on with the Lord. I would not go so far as to say that that is always the case; I am simply speaking from my own experience with people; and I have found that those who are unclear and hazy about matters like justification do tend not to get on in the spiritual life, and to get stuck in a rut, and indeed become more and more confused and mixed up as the days go by.

Well, then, to put on the breastplate of righteousness therefore means two things: first, for the man who has never come to grips with the gospel it means to be justified and accounted as righteous before God, and to know what that means; and secondly, for the man who has accepted Christ but knows little else it means to get down to basic study and get a right hold of the heart of the gospel and its deepest meaning. Now it is very impressive to realise that all too often nowadays evangelical ministry tends to be lacking in the solid teaching of former days, and that what we call 'devotional literature' so often does duty for the discipline of rich and substantial exposition of the Scriptures and the teaching of doctrinal truth. I strongly urge young believers to make a conscience of studying such doctrines. I shall always thank God that quite by chance—or was it chance?—one day many years ago I picked up a book on one of the barrows in Glasgow which has proved to be an absolute mine of treasure in doctrinal truth: Fisher's *Commentary on The Shorter Catechism*. Fisher was one of Thomas Boston's colleagues, one of the

Marrow-Men, one of the Seceders of the 18th century. This book has been not only nourishment to my soul and light to my understanding; it has been a breastplate to my heart, to guard me against the attacks of the enemy. One of the purposes of the teaching in these studies, which let it be admitted is often repetitive, is simply to instil a true and adequate knowledge of doctrine into those who will listen, that their lives might be shaped by it; never doctrine merely, but doctrine with life in it. You may recall what Paul says in Romans 6 when he writes, 'Ye used to be servants of sin, but now ye have obeyed from the heart that form of doctrine unto which you were delivered.' I think that is a very important statement—obeying from the heart the form of doctrine, the shape of teaching, unto which you were delivered. Now I believe that when that obtains in a believer's life he is thereby putting on the breastplate of righteousness.

Well, then, let us think of this: 'the Lord our righteousness, the righteousness of God.' The central passage in Romans, from chapter 3 on to chapter 5, speaks of this righteousness of God apart from the law which has been manifested in Jesus Christ and in the death that He died. Then Paul goes on in chapter 4 to say that this righteousness is imputed to us, and in chapter 5 makes it clear that it is received by faith alone. Now this is the heart of the gospel. What does it all mean? What does it mean that the righteousness of God should be imputed to us? Well, now, let us rehearse this whole theme from the beginning. Paul says in the opening chapter of

Romans that the gospel reveals the righteousness of God, and goes on to show why this is man's need, because man is basically unrighteous; he lacks righteousness, and therefore he cannot appear before God. Now to anybody who really thinks, this is the most important thing in all the world. The ultimate question for every man is, How do I stand before God ? This is the inescapable question, this is the only real question in life that matters. Now because man is unrighteous, he cannot appear before God; he is not right with God. Works cannot save him, as Paul is at pains to make clear : 'By the deeds of the law shall no flesh be justified in His sight.' This is a hard pill for many to swallow, because many seek to work their passage to heaven; in spite of all that the Scriptures say they have this sneaking hope that in the end, if they try hard enough, God will accept them. And Paul says, 'By the deeds of the law there shall no flesh be justified in His sight.'

But there are those who seem to think that justification means that God will make up what is lacking in our own righteousness; in other words, we do the best we can, and then what is lacking after that God will make up and see that all is well. This, of course, is a complete perversion of the truth. No man, said Jesus, putteth a new cloth on an old garment. Then there are those who think that God will have mercy on us if we are truly contrite and penitent before Him; but this is just as great a perversion of the gospel. We are not saved because we are sorry. We are not saved because we repent. There are no conditions to salvation. Salvation is free, unconditional.

To think of repentance as being a condition of salvation simply makes repentance a work by which we
are justified, i.e. something we do. We shall never be
justified by anything that we can do, because justification is something outside of us, apart from us alto-
gether. It is God that justifies, and justification is His
gift.

But the question arises, How can God justify sinners and still remain just? How can He do this without mocking the inviolable laws of the universe? The
answer the Scriptures give is: Through Jesus Christ
our Lord. In some way, Christ's death enables God to
justify the ungodly and still remain just Himself: It
is therefore in a true understanding of the meaning
of Christ's death that we arrive at a true estimate of
justification, and the ground of man's acceptance
with God. Now the Scriptures reveal God as Creator
and Law-giver, and as such He has a right to expect
from man His creature obedience to his laws, and
loyalty and devotion to his Person. But man has
sinned, and God has got neither obedience to His laws
nor loyalty or devotion to His Person; and this means
that over against man there are two set things: (1)
a broken law, and (2) a broken relationship. And
since man's unrighteousness, as Paul explains in
Romans 1, draws forth the wrath of God, that wrath
is revealed in a two-fold way: against sin as guilt (the
broken law), and against sin as lack of righteousness.
Therefore man has a two-fold need if he is to be put
right with God: he needs something to deal with his
guilt, and something to enable him to fulfil his obligations to God in terms of righteousness. And it is this

two-fold task which Christ takes upon Himself for our sakes: the provision of something to deal with our guilt, and something to enable us fulfil our obligations to God in terms of righteousness and loyalty and devotion to His Person.

Now the question of dealing with man's guilt is of course, as we know, the theme of many of our very greatest evangelical hymns; for example, that hymn, 'Man of Sorrows' with this wonderful second verse:

> *Bearing shame and scoffing rude,*
> *In my place condemned He stood;*
> *Sealed my pardon with His blood.*

The pardon of man's guilt sealed in the blood of Christ. We often hear contemptuous strictures being made upon the evangelistic phraseology, speaking about 'the blood' and all the rest of it. Now I freely admit that there is a good deal of unthinking speaking about the blood of Christ that had better not be done. But when you get down to the Scriptures, you cannot get away from it—you cannot have a gospel, you cannot have justification, except by blood. It was very salutary on one occasion a year or two ago to hear Professor T. F. Torrance of New College standing at the rostrum in the Assembly reminding the Fathers and Brethren that John Knox kept insisting that justification was by blood, 'justified by His blood' even more than the emphasis 'justified by faith', because that is the true objectivity of the gospel. Justification is by something outside of us, by the blood of Christ. Let us not be ashamed to speak of salvation by blood, rightly understood. Let us not be unthinking, let us not bandy holy words carelessly upon our lips; let us understand them; but let us recognise that our salvation resides in the blood that Jesus shed.

The Scriptures say that Christ suffered, the just for the unjust, that is to say, Christ stood in for us as our substitute, He took our place, taking upon Himself what was ours by reason of our sins. He was made sin for us, that we might become the righteousness of God in Him. You see? That is the breastplate. And when a man becomes the righteousness of God in Him he is clad in a breastplate that no arrow of the devil can penetrate. Now the essential thought in this connection is the sinlessness of Christ. In the Old Testament's sacrificial system, you will remember, it was always stressed that the animal victim must be spotless and without blemish; and the thought behind this is clear. Only a sinless one could take the sinner's place. A blemished one, animal or man, would stand responsible for its own blemish. And further, since sin, because it is sin against an infinite God, has something infinite about it—so infinite, in fact, that no mere finite human being could ever pay it—only an infinite person could stand in. And this is the marvel and the mystery of the gospel. To be real, atonement has to be made from man's side, because it is man who has done the wrong; but to be possible, it must come from God's side; and this dilemma is met in the mystery of the God-man. It is not God *per se* that atones for sin, but the God-man Jesus Christ, who meets both problems—the need for atonement to come from man's side, to be real, and for it to be possible, to come from God's. And in the God-man this dilemma is resolved, and Christ the God-man,—not God *per se*, but God in Christ—paid the penalty, and expiated the guilt of our sin.

But having said that, that is only, as it were, the negative side of Christ's work. God's wrath is stirred not only against man's guilt, but against his failure to give to God that which alone is well pleasing to Him, namely, holiness, answering to His own. And the same death that paid the price of sin and took away our own guilt was an offering to God, in a life laid down, of a holiness and a righteousness wholly satisfying to God and acceptable to Him. It is recorded of Christ that in Him was no sin. He not only did all things according to the will of God, he delighted to do God's will. Not merely obedience, but willing obedience, was the touchstone of His life. And this is what was so well-pleasing to God. It completely satisfied His righteous demands upon His creatures. And that life was laid on the altar by Christ for us. It was as if Christ was saying, 'Oh, God, take My life, holy, spotless, pure, lived every moment in fellowship with Thyself, take this for him, the unrighteous one. And He substituted His obedience, His righteousness for our unrighteousness; and by the obedience of One many are made righteous. That is the other aspect of the cross of Christ. You cannot separate them in fact, although one necessarily separates them in thought. It is the one death, Jesus did not die two deaths, but there were two aspects to it, and in that profound mystery atonement is made, and justification is made possible. Do you know the lines of the hymn,

> *Upon a life I have not lived,*
> *Upon a death I did not die—*
> *Another's life, Another's death—*
> *I stake my whole eternity.*

That is the heart of the gospel. That is what makes justification possible. Christ is made unto us righteousness like that, and what Christ did on the cross is imputed, reckoned, to us, put down to our account.

Now let us not be frightened of these unfamiliar words. Imputation is a word that has gone out of fashion, but let us think about it. People are prepared enough to adopt scientific terminology and other kinds of terminology, in work-a-day living, if they are interested in a subject. Let us be content with biblical terminology and learn what it means. To impute simply means to reckon, to put down to one's account. If I go up to a store in the town and buy something, I may not necessarily pay cash down, but I will say, Put it down to my account; and when I say that, the sum of money due to the store is imputed to me. It becomes my responsibility and I must meet it, it is mine. It is put down to my account, it is reckoned, and I pay the bill in due course. Now God imputes the righteousness of Christ, the finished work of grace, to us; He reckons it to us. This is how God can acquit sinners and justify men in His sight. And this is the bulwark of salvation; because when Christ's saving work is imputed to us, it is imputed once and for all, and for ever. It cannot change. This is the whole heart and essence of the Christian position, because, if it cannot change, then nothing Satan can do can disturb us. (But if we are not clear about this, he is going to demoralise us.) And to be immersed in this thinking, and overcome by it, by its grandeur and magnificence and glory, is to become impregnable against the assaults of the enemy. I could envisage a believer whose experience had been perhaps emotional and subjective, although quite real, being under attack by Satan and succumbing under the evil pressure to the belief that perhaps it had all been psychological and his imagination. Is not this exactly what happens in the homes of some young people who are converted, when their parents become the mouthpiece of Satan? Their parents say, 'Oh, it is just a religious phase. You will get over that; it will pass.' This is how Satan comes. Is it unknown that young believers become discouraged, and make shipwreck of faith by this very means? This is how Satan attacks. Now, if you have your breastplate on, and if you are standing in the consciousness of having this breastplate on, that is not going to disturb you. A man who has been gripped by the glory and reality of the justifying mercy of God, who has seen the wonder and awe of the divine transaction on the cross, that man is not going to be moved. We sing :

> I to the hills will lift mine eyes,
> From whence doth come mine aid.

Well, there are hills and hills, and there are mountain peaks in the holy Scriptures, and the great mountain peaks of Romans 3 are wonderful sources of aid for hard-pressed saints. Lift up your eyes to these hills when you are conscious of Satan's attacks, and derive your help from there. My safety cometh from the Lord, as the Psalmist said. I believe for a man's heart to be thrilled and awed by the glory of God's justification means to have on a breastplate that will make him impregnable and invincible against the onslaughts of the enemy.

Now as a necessary corollary to this, righteousness in the sense of integrity. For it is not possible but that a true experience of justification should lead to this integrity. One has only to examine the rest of the Epistle to the Romans, chapter 6 for example, where Paul in effect says, 'Know ye not that if you have been justified by faith you are crucified unto sin, you are dead to sin?' Justified men are crucified men, crucified to all that is untrue and all that is unrighteous and evil and unholy and unworthy. This is what justification means; and there is never a true experience of justification that does not lead to a complete break with sin. We have misunderstood it, we have lost the place somewhere, if justification for us means that we carry on in the same old way. Justification means being acquitted, and acquittal means that we go out free. A justified man is a man *freed* from sin. He is no longer in bondage to it. The law of the Spirit of life in Christ Jesus has made him free from the law of sin and death. He is free from sin. He is a man of integrity. He has been made true.

And there is an essential simplicity about life in

the justified state. It sheds the complications, the doubleness that we were speaking of in the last chapter in relation to truth in the meaning of sincerity. It is true that we are saved by faith alone; but faith that saves is never alone, but is ever accompanied with, and evidenced by, good works, works of integrity, characteristics of integrity. 'By their fruits ye shall know them,' said Jesus. To have on the breastplate of righteousness means not only that we rest by faith upon Christ's righteousness, but also that we allow those deep doctrines to work deeply in our hearts all manner of worthy and noble characteristics and qualities for the glory of God's great name. I have already quoted a verdict on the Calvinism of the 16th and 17th centuries in our own land, and the character, the integrity, that it produced in the lives of those who were gripped by it. This is it. This is why it seems to me so important that we start with the doctrinal aspect. We sometimes contrast the doctrinal with the practical, but that is really a misunderstanding of the situation. There is no biblical doctrine that is not practical. Any doctrine that is impractical is false doctrine. True biblical doctrine is the most practical thing in the world, and it produces practical qualities. The justification of God ultimately produces just men, righteous men, holy men. That is Paul's theme in the Epistle to the Romans. Imputed righteousness and experimental righteousness can never be separated in the lives of God's people.

Having therefore on the breastplate of righteousness you will be safeguarded from the attacks, the challenges, the arrows of doubt and confusion that the enemy delights to fire at us. And it may be that this is the simple and unequivocal answer to very real situations among us today, perhaps in young believers, perhaps in those not so young. Confused? Doubting? Get down to study, wrestle with it, wrestle with the Scriptures until you make them yield the truth that makes you free, and the righteousness that safeguards you against all the wiles of the devil.

4

THE PREPARATION OF THE GOSPEL OF PEACE

THIS IS the third part of the Christian armour. First of all we have a matter of interpretation to deal with. The phrase has a certain ambiguity about it. What do we mean by 'the preparation of the gospel of peace?' The Tyndale Commentary gives two different renderings. The first 'preparedness' in the sense of enabling the Christian warrior, and equipping the Christian warrior, to go forward carrying the good news of peace to others. I am sure that this particular interpretation is based on and certainly echoes, the words in Isaiah 52, 'How beautiful upon the mountains are the feet of them that preach the gospel of peace'—the idea of winged feet hastening, as it were, to preach the glad tidings. The other rendering is 'preparation' in the sense of 'a prepared foundation', that is, the knowledge of, and dependence on, the gospel that gives a man peace in his heart. This is a necessary equipment if he is to have a firm foothold in the conflict. And it seems to be the idea underlying the New English Bible rendering, 'Let the shoes on your feet be the gospel of peace, to give you firm footing.'

Now we need not spend much time discussing the

various interpretations, but it seems to me that in view of the general emphasis in the passage as a whole on standing—'Stand therefore, having your loins girt and your feet shod', rather than movement—walking or running—the second idea is more likely to be the point that Paul is making. It is for standing that you wear these gospel shoes, not for walking or running; and battle is the theme, not evangelism. And therefore to have the feet shod means to give us a firm foothold upon the rock that no assault will be able to shift. If you are standing on a slippery place, then the first good push is going to knock you off, especially if you have got on shoes that are prone to slip on slippery places. But if you are standing firm, and grounded firm, then the assaults will not budge you. And this part of the Christian armour, it seems to me, is to enable us to stand, and to stand firm, and not to panic or run away, knowing that the battle is not ours but God's. In other words, if we could use a modern colloquialism which has a very real relevance in this connection, these sandals, or shoes, are designed to keep the believer from getting cold feet!

Let me give you two illustrations from the Scriptures that make this point from opposite standpoints. First look at the story about Elisha at Dothan in 2 Kings 6. The young servant of the prophet was filled with dread at the sight of the enemy, but Elisha was calm and confident, standing firm and at peace, for he saw what the young man did not see. His feet were shod with the preparation of the gospel of peace. The gospel whose message is peace gave him an assurance that more than offset the danger and the crisis. That is the kind of thing Paul has in mind here: to be prepared as Elisha was prepared. 'Be like that,' he says, 'and all will be well.' Then you remember Elijah, on the other hand, after Mount Carmel, after the magnificent stand that he took there. His feet were shod with the preparation of the gospel of peace on Mount Carmel right enough; but then afterwards the reaction set in, and 1 Kings 19 shows the panic and the fear and the dread that this word here is designed to protect us against. Elijah forgot his shoes, and he was unnerved; and that such should have happened to a giant like Elijah is an indication to us just how important it is to be properly shod, and how real a possibility it is for us to be caught unawares and brought down as Elijah was, when he ran into the desert from the fury of Jezebel. If he had had on his gospel shoes, he would have stood firm and hurled defiance at the wicked queen, as he was well able to do, and as he had done on other occasions; but on this occasion he forgot his shoes, and he was lost.

We look now at two things: the nature of these gospel shoes or gospel sandals, and the nature of the attacks they are designed to ward off. And I think possibly it will be wiser for us too look at the nature of the attacks first. You see, Satan attacks us in different ways, at different times. We have suggested in the two previous chapters, for example, that there are times when Satan attacks us in the sphere of truth, and this is why it is so important to have our loins girt about with truth. In the last chapter we suggested there are times when Satan attacks our standing in Christ—justification—so as to bring confusion and doubt there, and that is why we have to be clad with the breastplate of righteousness. And sometimes Satan attacks the believer's peace. Now there are many causes of loss of peace. When a believer sins, he loses his peace. Repeated failure on the part of the believer can rob him of peace. Personal distress or involvement can rob a believer of his peace; and so on. It may be that Satan gets in his oar in all of these. But there is also a sphere of experience in which unaccountable disturbances sometimes assail the soul; disturbances for which there seems to be no rational explanation; strange, nameless dreads that steal upon the soul like a horror of great darkness. Now perhaps you do not know what I am talking about. If you do not, then thank God; but there are some here who know what I am talking about, and they know just how real these things are— these dreads, these oppressions of spirit, the sense of troubling, the sense of desolation, the terrible sense of being alone, of being forsaken by God. This is what David was meaning in the 22nd Psalm, and we should not forget that these words were spoken first by David, not by our Lord on the cross: 'My God, my God, why hast thou forsaken me?' We know their meaning in relation to Christ's use of them and His experience on the cross. But what did they mean for David when he spoke first, 'My God, my God, why has thou forsaken me?' Here was a man in a horror of great darkness. God had not forsaken him but he felt it.

And we recall Christian, in Bunyan's *The Pilgrim's Progress*, passing through the Valley of the Shadow, and these nameless pressures that crowded in upon his soul, robbing him of peace. Now, these are the attacks that Satan brings on the believer, and he can wreak havoc in the believer unless he is properly safeguarded, and for this he needs the shoes that Paul speaks of here. We sometimes sing:

> *When we in darkness walk,*
> *Nor feel the heavenly flame,*

'Then is the time to have our shoes on,' the hymn might say.

> *Then is the time to trust our God,*
> *And rest upon His name.*

But you cannot do that unless you have these gospel shoes on.

> *When darkness seems to veil His face,*
> *I rest on His unchanging grace.*

And, of course, these pressures do not need to be nameless either, for there are occasions when they can be given a very accurate name. In the story of Haman and Mordecai, you remember how Haman passed the gate of the King's palace and saw this Jew—this, as he thought, insolent Jew, who refused to bow and scrape before him as he passed. That is what robbed Haman of his peace. He was absolutely infuriated at this Mordecai. All that he had obtained in favour of the king was as nothing compared with the fact that this man refused to bow and scrape before him. That robbed him of his peace. It was his wounded conceit and pride; and sometimes this is what robs us of peace. Well, let us remember that Satan has a hand in this. Satan is attacking us, and we have to have that dealt with. And sometimes the intensity of this kind of attack tells us that there is something else as well as the old nature involved. Think of Haman: of course it was the old nature with him, but put the believer in that context. Is it unknown for believers to be churned up inside, irritated, made to think some awful thoughts about another, as the very sight of that other stirs things up in them? Is that unknown in believers? Of course it is not, and we must recognise that as well as the old nature at work there—and that is to be crucified—there is the old enemy as well, and he must be repulsed. And we must have on our gospel shoes.

Then there is that strange restlessness of spirit that sometimes assails us. I know, of course, that there is a restlessness of spirit that comes from God, and is often the precursor of a new movement, so far as our lives are concerned in relation to God's will, but that is not what I am referring to at the moment. There is that other restlessness of spirit that comes from Satan. It is Satan's work to bring a distemper of spirit upon us, and if we let him he will make havoc of our spiritual life and usefulness. This is something which we must recognise. There are many, many believers who are often assailed with this terrible restlessness. They cannot settle to anything. Watch them. They jump about from this to that and to the other. There is no consistency about them. There is no constancy. And they are being rendered ineffective in God's service. This is the work of Satan. One weekend I had a good deal of difficulty in my preparation for the pulpit. This is not an unknown thing in any minister's life, but that weekend I was particularly conscious of this kind of restlessness, and I knew perfectly well what was the cause of it. I knew I was under attack. There were times when I was prowling about like a wild beast in my study. I could not settle down in my chair and get down to the work, and I knew where that attack was coming from. This is the enemy, I kept saying to myself; I had to keep saying it to myself. This is the kind of thing I mean. Now there is only one way to deal with this. It is to put on your gospel shoes and stand fast and not yield an inch. Stand, with your feet shod with the preparation of the gospel of peace. That is the kind of attack we are thinking about here.

Now look at the nature of the provision. I said at the beginning of this chapter that the interpretation which speaks in this way, to give us a firm foothold upon the rock that no assault will be able to shift, is what Paul is getting at here. Now putting on your shoes does not mean that the assaults will stop. They do not. Putting on your shoes means that you will be able to stand against them. That is the provision. God does not promise ever that the assaults of the enemy will stop. We are never guaranteed this kind of ease in the Christian life, but we are guaranteed that, if we put on our shoes, we will be able to stand against them. The knowledge of, and dependence upon, the gospel that gives peace in the heart, is the necessary equipment that we need, if we are to have a firm foothold in the conflict. This is the preparedness that we require; this is the divine equipment.

When we speak like this, you see how closely this is linked with earlier parts of the armour; for peace flows from justification—being justified by faith we have peace with God—and justification is the act by which we receive the righteousness of Christ, by faith, as it is imputed to us.

Now the first thing we have to say here, and indeed the most important and all-comprehensive thing that we can say in this matter, is that to have our feet shod with the preparation of the gospel of peace is to recognise the completeness of our position in Christ, and what we are in Him; to recognise and to remember, by a lively exercise of faith, where the gospel has placed us. This is basic. Our position in Christ is far above all principality and power, as Paul puts it in Ephesians I. That is our position. Christ has spoiled principalities and powers, and the battle is already ours. Thanks be to God who giveth us the victory. So it is therefore a question of appropriating, and making our own in practical experience, what is already ours in Him, and what He has already given us. Paul says in Colossians, 'Let the peace of God rule in your hearts.' It is already there, he says; allow it to do its gracious work and exercise its guardian function, and take over, when these dark disturbances threaten you. Now this is the most practical thing in the world. Put yourself into that situation which I have just described—the restlessness of spirit, or the nameless dread that is pressing down upon you, or the darkness. In such a situation one tends to fear the worst. One tends to panic. One tends to lose heart. Now, says Paul, let the peace of God rule. Let it exercise, allow it to exercise, its guardian function in you. Allow it to take over. Say to God's peace—and remember He is our peace— 'Go on, take over now; this is the moment I need you to work.' If this thing does not work in a real situation it is of no use to anybody; it is a dead loss. It has got to work. We have got to be able with confidence to say, 'Go on, peace. You are there; take over; guard my heart from this. Go on now; do your work. That is what you are for.' This is how we must speak.

Let me illustrate it. Think of the episode in *The Pilgrim's Progress*, (I am assuming that you have read the book, but I am astonished at the numbers of people who have never done so! Next to the Bible, there is no book more important for a believer to know well than *The Pilgrim's Progress*) in which Christian came to the Palace Beautiful, and outside the palace gates there were two fierce lions. Mistrust and Timorous, his two companions, both turned back through fear of these lions. Watchful, the porter, said to Christian, 'Keep in the midst of the path and no hurt shall come to thee', and Christian went forward; he heard the lions roar, but they did him no harm. Now how was this? The lions were chained! And to know that made all the difference in the world.

In a real situation it would be something of an ordeal to go forward even if the lions were chained and you knew it, but it would be possible. But not to know it would make turning back a foregone conclusion, would it not? Now this is the point. This lion, who is attacking us, is chained. Keep in the midst of the path and no hurt shall come to you. The devil has a chain on him. This bears witness to the reality of the divine sovereignty. Satan can do nothing except by permission of God—nothing. And if we get that drummed into our hearts and spirits, then it is going to mean a tremendous thing for us. Peace in the midst of battle—this is the great paradox in the believer's life and in the Christian faith.

I want to give you three thoughts in particular which I believe will prove useful as specific instances or applications of the basic idea of recognising and remembering our position in Christ and what the gospel of peace gives us.

First of all, the gospel of peace gives us an assurance of our heavenly Father's presence.

> *When we in darkness walk,*
> *Nor feel the heavenly flame,*

it is precisely at that moment that we doubt His presence, that we feel He has forsaken us. 'My God, my God, why has thou forsaken me?' Now there are all sorts of instances in human experience in which that feeling becomes terribly real. You feel that God has absolutely abandoned you. The gospel of peace gives us an unfailing assurance of the Father's presence. 'That shalt call His name Emmanuel, which is, God with us.' That is what Christmas is about. And when Jesus ascended to the right hand of the Majesty on high, His very last words were, 'Lo, I am with you always, even unto the end of the world.' It is a matter of standing on the faithful word of God against all the evidence of our senses, against all the evidence of our experience. The darkness is enveloping us. There is absolutely no movement in our hearts, spiritually speaking. We cannot pray, we cannot sing, we cannot read the Scriptures. Everything is gone. But the gospel of peace comes to us and says, He is there, by your side. 'Lord, open the young man's eyes that he may see.' And behold the mountain was filled with horses and chariots of fire. Assurance of our Father's presence.

Do you remember how it was with the apostle Paul when he went to Corinth? This is a great encouragement, because Paul was not a feckless believer; he walked close with God. But there was an occasion—indeed there were many occasions in his experience when he felt this same desolation of spirit, crushing down upon him, and one of these occasions was in Corinth. Perhaps he was tired; it was towards the end of his second missionary journey, and when you come within a few months of your furlough you are very tired and you are very weary, and spiritual feelings are certainly not on the ascendant. And on that occasion Paul felt absolutely bleak and desolate. He felt so alone in Corinth, amidst all the iniquity about him, and God came to him and said, 'Be not afraid, hold not thy peace, for I am with thee and no man will set on thee to hurt thee.' That is what the gospel of peace gives us—an assurance of the Father's presence.

And, what is more, it gives us a glorious assurance of our Father's care and love. Now this is not something that could ever be exaggerated in the importance it has for the believer. I have often thought it is very significant that when the apostle Peter speaks of the devil going about like a roaring lion, seeking whom he may devour (and we have got to resist him, steadfast in the faith), he prefaces that word with one of the most gloriously comforting verses in the whole of the Bible: 'Casting all your care upon him; for he careth for you. Be sober, be vigilant; because your adversary, the devil . . .' But it does not matter about your adversary the devil if that is true! 'Casting all your care upon him; for he careth for you.' And, quite simply, we shall be able to resist the devil, steadfast in the faith, standing firm with our feet shod, if only we are sure of our Father's love and care.

Lack of this assurance and awareness is the source of a great deal of failure and spiritual breakdown in the Christian life. Why do we find so many bitter people among Christians? So many spiteful people, so many difficult people, so many who are easily offended? Well, you know, at the root of that kind of problem there is a deep underlying sense of insecurity and inferiority, and at the root of that is a lack of love. People whose lives have been touched by love are not inferior, or insecure, or easily offended, or difficult or bitter. Love brings contentment. Love is an expansive thing, and, when the consciousness of the divine love really comes home to a soul, these thing go out. This is something that we must always remember. If we allowed a Father's love to sink into our hearts, so many of these distressing and embarrassing symptoms would just disappear from our lives. The Book of Ruth, it seems to me, gives us a wonderful example of this, in the character of Boaz. Read the book and see this man Boaz; see if you agree with me when I say he is presented to us as a noble, generous, kind, good, lovable, honourable man, pure and chaste as a child. But the question I put is this, What might he have been? Because, you see, his background was this—his mother was a harlot, and what an inheritance and background he must have had! All that might have combined to give him a grudge at life and make him bitter—lovelessness, lack of care, the shadow and the slur of illegitimate birth following him all through life. How understandable it would have been if Boaz had turned out to be a hard and mean and self-seeking man, with all kinds of complexes. But grace broke into that life, and broke the inevitable consequence of such an upbringing, and made a man of him. Why? He found, and he was found by, a Father's love; and the Book of Ruth simply breathes this.

This is a very useful corrective today. We are very grateful for all the psychiatric knowledge and interpretation which has thrown so much light on difficulties of human personality and so on; but we must always be careful lest we become too sold on that, because the tendency does seem to be that one excuses anything and everything because of background. There are many believers who excuse their own difficulties and their own problems, excuse them to themselves and to other people, and blame them upon their background. 'It was my upbringing; it was something that happened when I was three and a half. I cannot help it. I am not responsible if I am mean and spiteful, if I am difficult to get on with; it was something in my background. It is not my fault.' Let us recognise this : the grace of God can break into anything; the grace of God can heal human lives. This is the point of the gospel. Let us not lose sight of it. When we are so enamoured of psychiatric theory, let us not lose sight of this. The gospel of Jesus Christ is the power of God unto salvation. It saves, it redeems a man from his difficulties, from his problems, from his inhibitions, from his inferiority complexes. There is no excuse. Let the grace of God attack them. And that will be an end of them. Boaz is a case in point. The son of a harlot. You know, some people never seem to be able to live down their family history. Let me say something. Come to terms with it, accept it, say, 'All right, that is what I came from, but God has claimed me, and there is nothing too hard for the Lord.' Look at Boaz. This is what the gospel of peace gives us—the assurance of the Father's love and care.

And, of course, we must not forget this. The gospel of peace gives us peace, peace with God in the objective sense, giving us a new standing before God, justified by His glorious mercy. It also gives us the peace of God that passes all understanding. I have mentioned the nameless fears, the dreads, the clouds that have no rational explanation. They are nameless, they cannot be understood. Well, the answer to them is the peace that cannot be understood, the peace that passes all understanding. That is what God gives. You know that wonderful word in Isaiah about 'peace like a river'. It is a very eloquent simile, is it not? But have you ever thought of following it through and applying it? Tease it out and see what it means—peace like a river. Do you know that beautiful piece of music from 'My Country' by Smetana, the Czech composer, in which he traces the River Vltava from its source right down to the sea, and tries to paint in music all the various moods of the river: the tiny rivulet trickling down the rocks and the hills at the source, the long meandering reaches, the fast-flowing currents, the deep movements? You see, a river is not just one bit. It has not got one mood; it has many moods. And so has the peace of God. The peace of God is not a formless thing; it is many-coloured. The peace of God in one context can be bubbling over with gaiety, like a stream cascading down the rocks; and in another context it can be deep and mysterious. We do not see any movement at all although the water is flowing swiftly for all that. And in another context the peace of God can be like the meandering reaches of a river, slowly, almost lazily crawling down. The peace of God has many moods.

And another thing. If you throw the branch of a tree into a river, does that stop the river's flow? Of course not. What the river does is to bear it along effortlessly, and push it into the side, and old man river goes rolling along! There are some people of whom it could be said that it takes very little to disturb their peace. We speak of throwing a little cog into a machine and that disrupts the machine, but that is a different metaphor, and it is not like that with the peace of God. You can throw a big tree into the river of God's peace, and all that will happen is that it will be eased down to the edge, to the bank. And even very great disturbances are not big enough to hinder the peace of God. When it is the real peace of God, that peace will take the great trunk of a tree and firmly push it into the side of the bank. Or take another idea—that great rock in the middle of the river bed. Does that stop the river? No, it is immovable; but what happens is that the river simply flows round both sides of it and goes peacefully on its way. And there are things like that in human experience; they are immovable, they are there for the duration—a sorrow, it may be, a tragedy, a thorn in the flesh—it is not going to be moved. But the peace of God is not held up by it; it flows round both sides, and goes right on. That is what God can do. That is what the gospel of peace can give. And with these shoes on, we will stand like Elisha. 'Lord, open his eyes.' God's word has been shafts of light into our experience, to tell us about our 'gospel shoes'. Get on your shoes, man; that will stop you getting cold feet. You will stand, and may God bless you.

5

THE SHIELD OF FAITH

THE NEXT piece of Christian armour that we study is the shield of faith, and concerning this Paul says, 'Above all, take the shield of faith.' Now this phrase 'above all' has been variously interpreted. Some take it to mean 'most especially', others take it to mean 'over all' with reference to position, 'above all the rest of the armour'. Some take it to mean 'in all things', that is to say 'in all duties, in all enterprises, in all temptations' and so on. Now the phrase could mean all these and I do not see why we should not take it to mean all these. There is certainly some ground for taking the first rendering, 'most especially take the shield of faith'. For not only does the shield of faith take the central position in this catalogue of Christian armour, with three parts mentioned before it and three after it, but also it is the one piece of armour which is spoken of especially as having a particular function and result. 'Loins girt about with truth' : that is a plain and simple statement without any rider added to it; 'breastplate of righteousness'; a simple statement; 'preparation of the gospel of peace' : a simple statement. But now, 'the shield of faith, wherewith ye shall be able to quench all the fiery darts of the wicked one'. Then, 'helmet of salvation', 'sword of the Spirit, which is the word of God', 'praying always', the weapon of all-prayer. That is the only one which has this significant rider, and this in itself should surely give it an especial place: 'most especially the shield of faith'. At the same time, however, we can see also the force of the rendering 'over all' as to position, for the shield is a movable commodity. You can move it to cover the loins, or the breast, or the legs, or the feet, or the head; and in effect this shield provides double armour, covering armour that is already there. It is reinforcement to all the others, and from the spiritual point of view this is very important. Loins girt about with truth; but what is the use of truth if we have not faith? Breastplate of righteousness; but what is the use of that if we have not faith? And so on.

Now the shield referred to here is the big, massive shield, the scholars tell us, used by Roman infantry, 4 ft high and 2½ ft broad, and it is the kind of shield that could cover the whole body with ease. Interestingly enough, one of my commentaries says that the Greek word is used in Homer to mean a stone put against a door to block it or to shut it. Now that to me is a very suggestive thought. The shield of faith closes and blocks doors against the enemy's arrows. This is a great thought. A closed door. The shield of faith is, of course, the shield which is faith, or the shield which faith provides. Faith is the shield. One commentator has said this: 'It is that faith of which Christ is the object, which receives Him as the Son of God and the Saviour of men; it is the faith which is the substance of things hoped for, and the evidence of things unseen.' Another says, 'That faith whereby we resolutely rely on God and His word for deliverance from temptation. The true safeguard in the evil day lies ever not in introspection, but in that look wholly outward and Godward, which is the essence of faith.' Now, clearly, the two important considerations here are, first, the nature of faith as a shield, and, secondly, the nature of the fiery darts of the wicked one, that is to say, what kind of experiences are referred to in this phrase, 'the fiery dart of the wicked', so far as the believer is concerned. And, once again, I think we should look at the latter first, the kind of experiences, and then we shall look at the nature of the provision that is made in the divinely given shield of faith.

Well, then, what is the nature of these attacks of Satan? Once again we see how closely linked this is to what we have already studied, and perhaps particularly in the last chapter; indeed much of what I said then about the kind of attack that is made on the believer's peace could with equal truth be said here in relation to the fiery darts of the wicked. However, the particular emphasis is on the *fiery* darts of the wicked, and this has something particular to say to us. The picture is from ancient warfare: arrows or like missiles, darts, around which combustible materials were fastened and ignited were then fired against the enemy. In the stories of cowboys and Indians that we used to love as boys we read of the Indians firing upon the covered wagons with the flaming arrows and setting them ablaze instantly. Now the characteristic of these arrows is their swiftness, their un-

expectedness, their immediate effect, and their deadliness. And, of course, there is a double deadliness in
them, for they pierce as well as set on fire.

Now how do we relate all this to the believer's
experience? What happens in a believer when he is
attacked by the fiery darts of the wicked one? Well,
I think we can look at this in several ways. In the previous chapter I spoke of the darkness of nameless
depression that sometimes settles upon a believer's
soul. But here is something different from that, but
just as terrible. I refer to spiritual darkness and doubt.
This is a pall of spiritual darkness that not so much
makes a man feel like David, as if he were forsaken
by God, as to make him doubt seriously his own salvation, and even to doubt the existence of God. Now
I am speaking not of unbelievers and tendencies in
them towards atheism, but believers born of the Spirit
of God, under attack by the evil one, and coming
perilously near to practical atheism in their minds
and in their hearts because of this terrible darkness
that comes down.

Let me illustrate. Here is a young servant of God,
a minister of the gospel. It is Saturday evening and he
is due to be preaching next day. His preparation is
complete, he has worked hard and diligently at his
sermon, and he is now ready as to the preaching
matter. This man is an evangelical. He loves his
work. His heart and soul are in it, and he has not been
without fruit in his ministry, as others would be
able to testify. And on this Saturday evening, warm
at heart in the expectation of blessing the following
day, he is, as it were, feeding his own soul on an

article in a magazine, written by a well-known preacher (this is a true story; this is fact), and finding this article helpful, stimulating and spiritually refreshing. Then a phrase in the article catches his eye particularly. It starts a train of thought, a stab of dismay and dread assails his spirit, and in a matter of minutes his whole inner soul is a raging inferno of doubt. He is doubting his own salvation. He is doubting God Himself, the very existence of God, and the whole business of the gospel seems utterly unreal and fictitious to him, in a matter of minutes. And for days that storm rages. He preaches next day with the raging inferno within him, with this terrible thing tormenting him all the way through. And it takes terrific toll of all mental, emotional, and physical energy. It nearly prostrates him. Now what is this that has happened to him? This is one of Satan's fiery darts, and it can happen as swiftly and unexpectedly and out of the blue as that.

But there are other darts, for that is only one instance. Let me remind you of some of the insights that we find in the Book of Job particularly in chapters 9 and 16. Let me just read some verses. Listen to this, from the R.S.V. You remember the situation. Job is in a terrible darkness, he is groping and wrestling with something nameless. 'God will not turn back his anger; beneath him bowed the helpers of Rahab. How then can I answer him, choosing my words with him? Though I am innocent, I cannot answer him; I must appeal for mercy to my accuser.' Notice the words; he is speaking of God. 'If I summoned and he answered me, I would not believe that he was listening to my voice. For he crushes me with a tempest, and multiplies my wounds without cause; he will not let me get my breath, but fills me with bitterness. If it is a contest of strength, behold him! If it is a matter of justice, who can summon him? Though I am innocent, my own mouth would condemn me; though I am blameless, he would prove me perverse. I am blameless; I regard not myself; I loathe my life. It is all one; therefore I say, he destroys both the blameless and the wicked. When disaster brings sudden death, he mocks at the calamity of the innocent. The earth is given into the hand of the wicked; he covers the faces of its judges.' And then this: 'If it is not he, who then is it?'

Now let me explain what is happening here. Job is passing through a terrible experience in which his mind is confused very deeply and very radically. He is convinced that God is judging him and accusing him, he is saying all those terrible things about God; and then in a momentary gleam he says, 'Well, if it is not God, who is it? The answer is, It is Satan. But the point I am making is that Job thought it was God. This is something that happens in the lives of believers. They pass through strange and frightening and terrifying experiences and they feel that God is doing this to them. And sometimes they never have any gleam of insight into the possibility that it might not be God at all, but Satan. One of the most fruitful insights in this wonderful Book of Job for me has been to see this glimmering of hope kindling in Job's mind. He speaks of an accuser, he feels that God is accusing him relentlessly, piling tempest after tempest upon him; and this is what is so terrible to this man, that his God whom he has loved and revered and honoured and obeyed should turn out to be this kind of God. And only occasionally does he get a glimmer of thought that perhaps it is not God. I think this is quite the most terrifying experience a believer can ever pass through. And this is my point. Often, Satan's darts come like this, purporting to come from God, and make utter desolation of the believer's heart. Job says earlier on, 'The arrows of the Almighty are sticking in me', but what if it was not the arrows of the Almighty, what if it was the fiery darts of the wicked one? That would explain so much in the Book of Job. Indeed we have the first two chapters of Job to tell us that they *are* the fiery darts of the wicked one that Job thought were God's arrows.

I say that sometimes this afflicts a believer and it comes to him purporting to be from God, when all the time it is from the enemy; but in the confusion between the two, utter desolation comes to him— the inward promptings, for example, that come to him as he is intent on following Christ, promptings that lay imperious demands on him, dazing him with their sheer arbitrariness and unpredictability, until God appears to be a harsh and arbitrary and un- lovely tyrant. Now it is easy to say, 'How could any- body be taken in by this?' but the fact of the matter is, many are taken in by this. And if you have not ever been through this experience you have no right to say, How could anybody be taken in by this. Wait till it comes upon you, and you will find out how people can be taken in by it. And it is not a simple thing to discern, when you are in the thick of it, for, of course, it is often aided and abetted by unwise spiritual teaching of the sort that insists that all inward promptings and demands are to be obeyed immediately and without question, otherwise a man is not truly consecrated. My early Christian life was shattered by just this kind of exhortation that I found in a book of readings. It said, 'Obey instantly, no matter how strange or unusual or crazy the command may seem to be; obey it instantly.' And I wanted to be right with God; I had given my life to Him, and I wanted to be obedient. And these imperious demands came upon my soul and nearly drove me out of my mind before I discovered that they were not the voice of God but the fiery darts of the wicked. You see, this kind of spiritual counsel forgets the scripture which says, 'Beloved, try the spirits whether they be of God.' Try the spirits!

Now my whole concern in these studies is to be as practically helpful as possible, and I want to illustrate in order to show the kind of thing I mean. Here is a young engaged Christian couple whom God has brought together, and it is clearly a divinely arranged match. They are well suited to one another, they are deeply in love with one another, they are dedicated to Christ and to His service. And then the girl has a sudden, inward prompting and conviction that she should break off the engagement; she feels that God is saying to her, 'You must break this off.' You can easily see the ferment and torment in the girl's heart, and in his heart too when he learns about it. Now this has happened, on at least two occasions in my ministry, in the past few years. She wrestles with this thing. Has not God brought them together? Did not the guide-lines seem to be clear and unequivocal? The answer to all these questions was, Yes. But there is this constant, nagging, imperious word, 'Break it off, break it off; it is not for you.' And she has no peace and no rest until she breaks it off, and breaks her heart, and breaks his heart. When she does so she has a measure of peace in her conscience, and that seems to confirm to her that she has done the right thing, sore as it has been. The only thing is that, a little time later, another imperious command insinuates itself into her life about something else, the same kind of persecuting voice. And on and on it goes. It was not God who was speaking to her at all. This was Satan. This was one of the fiery darts of the wicked, and that voice needed to have been tried to see whether it was of God. And it is part of a discerning pastoral ministry to understand that this can happen, to take steps to expose the enemy, and to get people to use the shield of faith whereby the fiery darts of the wicked can be quenched.

Do not misunderstand me. That is simply an example. I am not suggesting for a moment that this is the way Satan usually comes to young people. It is one way that he sometimes uses with some people, that is all. But it illustrates the point—the fiery darts of the wicked, out of the blue. Of course, I say this without prejudice. Sometimes God does come to an engaged couple and says, 'Now this is wrong.' But when He does so, He does not bulldoze them into action; He is persuasive. The voice of the Spirit is a gentle voice, full of sweet reasonableness; and if we are prepared to listen to the voice of the Spirit He will convince us. He will carry our judgment with Him. That is the fundamental difference. I have spoken to countless people, not all of them young people either, who have been misled, and who have nearly made shipwreck of their spiritual lives by being misled in this way. Try the spirits, whether they be of God. We have to learn to recognise the voice of God and distinguish it from the voice of the devil. My sheep, says Jesus, know my voice. Do you think our blessed Lord would come to two of His children, whose hearts are full of love for Him and for one another, and bludgeon them, and bulldoze them, into doing a thing like that? Jesus does not speak to people like that. He just is not like that. That is what Job was getting glimmerings of—this harsh, peremptory voice that was accusing him so much that he began to say, 'Is this God? and if it is not, who is it?' Chapters 1 and 2 of Job tell us who it is. It is Satan. Try the spirits whether they be of God.

Then, of course, there are these sudden temptations that come like blazing arrows. We all know that temptation is the common lot of man, but we also know that there are some temptations the suddenness of which and the intensity of which make it obvious that they are directly from the enemy. The rapidity with which they start off a conflagration in the soul is sometimes absolutely terrifying, like the sudden devastating squalls and storms that arise on the Sea of Galilee—one minute the sun is shining and the next minute the boat is in the grip of a terrible storm that threatens to overturn it, and bring it down to the watery depths of the sea. Sometimes Christian life is like that. Well now, we must recognise these, and also the times that they come.

Forgive me for speaking of my own experience again; I am not trying to be personal, but it does make the point. I know, for example, that there are certain times in my life when this is much more likely to happen that at other times. A Saturday night, a Sunday morning, before I am due to preach the Word—that is when I become a target, and that is when fearsome, sudden temptations could very well assail me. And I must learn to recognise that they are coming not from an unsanctified nature, although in all conscience my nature is very unsanctified, but from the enemy from without—darts being fired at me, to stir up a fire, and render me inoperative at a crucial moment in the work of God. Now read that into your own situation, your Sunday school class, it may be, or some piece of Christian service you are engaged in, and it is precisely then that the enemy attacks.

Then there are these terrible thoughts that are injected into the mind—foul thoughts, impure thoughts, blasphemous thoughts, malignant thoughts, ugly thoughts, sceptical thoughts—again at particular times—in your quiet time with God, when you are reading the Scriptures, when you are worshipping in His house. Have some of you noticed that evil thoughts are worst when you are in God's house? Is that a terrible thing to say? It is very understandable to me. When you are praying? And, of course, the same applies to wandering thoughts. We are all afflicted with wandering thoughts when we are praying. Satan sees to that. But so often it is the uglier ones, the fiery ones, that start up a flame within your heart—the fiery darts of the wicked one. There are so many more things we could say.

But let us think of the nature of the provision that is made for us. 'Above all, taking the shield of faith, wherewith ye shall be able . . .' now notice the promise; notice how confident Paul is—'ye shall be able. Provided ye take the shield, the battle is yours—ye shall be able to quench all the fiery darts of the wicked.' Now, remember the size of the shield— $4 \times 2\frac{1}{2}$. Even the most diligent enemy is not going to get by that size of a shield if you have got it up before you.

But first of all, and part of the operation of faith, is the need for recognition that we are under attack. This is absolutely essential. As long as ever we are not conscious of what is going on, as long as ever we are talking like Job, and thinking it is God that is doing this, when it is the devil, then nothing is going to be accomplished, no battles are going to be won, no victories are going to be achieved. Recognise, study this subject, think about it, recognise the possibility that your problem today may be simply the fiery darts of the wicked one. Recognise the possibility. And then application : faith must operate instantly, because they come so swiftly. And indeed, the shield must be up before they start coming. It is too late to put up the shield when the arrow is stuck in your breast and burning fiercely.

Now it is faith in its fundamental sense that Paul, I think, has in mind here—saving faith, faith in Christ, justifying faith, with all its glorious implications. If we study the words in the Old Testament and the New for 'faith' and 'trust', we find that the characteristic emphases in both the Old and New Testaments are all words of committal, when we give ourselves utterly over to Christ: to stay oneself upon, to take refuge in, to lean upon, to cling to, to rest upon, to believe 'into', the Lord Jesus Christ. And if we are casting ourselves utterly upon God, we are laying hold upon the infinite resources that are in Him for our help and deliverance. Wesley's words in 'Jesus, Lover of my soul' express this very beautifully and very accurately. Listen:

> *Other refuge have I none;*
> *Hangs my helpless soul on Thee;*
> *Leave, ah! leave me not alone;*
> *Still support and comfort me.*
> *All my trust on Thee is stayed,*
> *All my help from Thee I bring;*
> *Cover my defenceless head*
> *With the shadow of Thy wing.*

That is a man who is taking the shield of faith, faith is operating, faith in the mighty Christ of God; not faith in our faith, but faith in Christ who is the object of faith. Faith is faith in a Person; we repose our confidence in Him alone. But you say, how do you exercise trust in a Person you are no longer able to believe in? What of this young servant of God, for example, who has been attacked by Satan, and in a matter of moments his faith is gone, his assurance of salvation is gone, his feeling that there is a God is gone? How does this work with him? Well, I believe there is only one thing to do—to affirm faith in the bare Word of God, against all the feelings and convictions of your heart. It is written! He that cometh to God must believe that He is. Stand upon the Word of God.

> *Standing on the promises that cannot fail*
> *While the howling storms of doubt and fear assail,*
> *By the living word of God I shall prevail*
> *Standing on the promises of God.*

Do not be afraid to do so; it will be strong enough to hold you up. Stand on the promises!

I have a Bible at home which was with me in my early days of travail and shattered faith, and there are some chapters in the Book of Isaiah, especially in the second half of that wonderful prophecy, that have been stained and marked with tears, tears of despair and tears of hope, as God has given me a word to stand on and I have clung to it, and stumbled on to it, and have tried to stand firm, when all the powers of hell seemed to be raging round my heart and spirit and head. Do that. It is written. Remember this: justification means that God has turned a reconciled face towards us once and for all. He cannot accuse us. Satan is the accuser of the brethren, God does not accuse those who are in Christ. He chastises them, that is a different matter, but He does not accuse in the way that Job is speaking of accusations and tempests being hurled upon him. 'If it is not He, who then is it?' And the answer is, it is Satan.

And what about these peremptory, harsh voices within us? Well, we must first recognise the possibility of other voices than that of God, and resolutely refuse them in Christ's name, maintain an attitude of faith in our hearts, faith in the God whose character we know in Christ, and assert this against the clamant, imperious demands within us, remembering John the Apostle's words, 'Beloved if our hearts condemn us, God is greater than our hearts.' Now, that is a word for you! This, of course, is the whole point. In a believer's experience, in this respect, even if he discerns, however faintly, that there may be a possibility of Satan speaking these words, and not God, there is the awful fear, 'What if it is not Satan? What if it is God?' Well, let faith operate. Let faith give you clear eyes—look up to Him; look at what He is. Use your imagination, to put it in another way. Imagine Jesus is sitting there in the chair in front of you, and try to put these words from these voices on His lips and see if they fit, and you will find that there is an incongruity which is basic and fundamental. And in that realisation you will have deliverance; you will say with amazed wonder 'My Jesus does not speak like that, with that voice!' Beloved, if our heart condemn us, God is greater than our heart. Go against that voice; dare to disobey it, for it is not God speaking, but

Satan. Assert your faith in God and demand that you will have a real and normal Christian life—not one troubled by these blackmailing voices.

Now as I said in the last chapter, perhaps you do not know what I am talking about. If you do not, thank God. But if you do, take this from God today. This may be your deliverance. Faith tells us what we are and who we are in Christ, and reminds us of the kind of persons we are by the grace of God: by the grace of God we are no longer the kind of person that can be overcome by temptation. We are the kind of person in Christ that can look temptation in the eye and say, 'No, begone; I refuse to have truck with you. I am a new man in Christ, and I refuse these things.' Thrust them out. Be like the policeman on point-duty, and put up that hand and say, 'Halt.' And wave on this other line of traffic, the holy traffic, and let your mind be overrun by that, and keep that other one there. Technically, a policeman could keep that line of traffic standing there all day long; they dare not go against the white-gloved hand. My friends, we have something greater than a white-gloved hand. We have a nail-pierced hand by us. Raise that hand, and say to the enemy, 'Look, begone.'

And one final word. I spoke about cowboys and Indians and the blazing arrows fired at the caravans dry as tinder, and at the thatched roofs of the settlers' houses. Well, you know, a blazing arrow will never ignite a wet thatch. Water your shield with the water of the Word and with prayer. Dowse it with the Word and prayer. Saturate it and Satan's darts will simply fizzle out. Oh, they will stick, but they will fizzle out. And there is nothing in the world so gloriously satisfying as to see one of the fiery darts of the wicked fizzling out on the shield of faith that has been saturated with the Word and prayer. Let your faith be awakened to take its true place in your experience. Water it with the Word and with prayer, and you shall be able to quench all the fiery darts of the wicked one.

6

THE HELMET OF SALVATION

THIS IS the next piece of Christian armour, or, as Paul puts it in 1 Thessalonians 5. 8, 'for an helmet the hope of salvation'. The commentators point out that the verb 'take' has the force of 'receive', and again, as in the previous parts, what is stressed is the givenness of the armour. It is the gift of God to His people. Once again there is a reference to the passage in Isaiah 59, which depicts the divine warrior, who wears the helmet of salvation, as being the worker of deliverance, clothed and armed with his great purpose to bring deliverance to his people. And the Christian warrior wears this same helmet in the sense of being the receiver and the possessor of deliverance, clothed and armed in the victory of the Lord. It is the Lord's salvation that is given to us. This is the idea.

Now, we need to notice once again the importance of the imagery here. A helmet guards the head and protects the eyes. This part of Christian armour, therefore, is obviously something for the mind, and the thoughts. And the meaning, in brief, appears to be something like this: a mind constantly preoccupied with thoughts of our great salvation is kept safe from the onslaughts of the enemy. This is the thesis that is before us now. We could collate an in-

teresting number of scriptural verses in this connection. You remember, for example, that glorious
word in Isaiah 26, 'Thou wilt keep him in perfect
peace, whose mind is stayed on Thee.' This is someone who has his helmet on. Peter says in his first
Epistle, 'Gird up the loins of your mind.' Paul says in
Philippians 4. 7, 'The peace of God . . . shall keep your
hearts and minds.' This is the helmet of salvation.
And as Paul goes on in the following verse, 'Whatsoever things are lovely and of good report, think on
these things.' And as we sometimes sing:

> *With salvation's walls surrounded,*
> *Thou mayest smile at all thy foes.*

That, then, is the idea in this part of the armour.

When dealing with earlier parts of the Christian
armour, we found ourselves almost inevitably turning our thoughts first of all to the nature of the
attacks that may be envisaged, then to the nature of
the provision that is offered by God for these attacks,
and we will do that again now.

So we think first of all of the possible nature of
the enemy's attacks, for which the helmet of salvation is the divine answer and divine provision. Well,
if the helmet is for the head, to guard the mind and
the eyes, then that is the realm we need to think
about, in relation to the enemy's attacks. First of all,
then, attacks on the mind. It is not for nothing that
Satan is sometimes called in the Scriptures 'The
Destroyer', for sometimes his aim seems to be to
destroy the believer's sanity. A notable instance of

this is seen in the story of 1 Samuel of King Saul, that towering giant of a man, who stood head and shoulders above his fellows, whose early life prospered so greatly and promised so much in the things of God, but who through disobedience opened the door to evil influences, to evil spirits that worked a progressive disintegration of his mind and whole personality, until he ended his life in mental disorder and ruin. Here is a man, a magnificent specimen of manhood, as the Scripture goes out of its way to point out to us; a man among men, and somehow, tragically—we are not concerned with the why and wherefore at the moment—he became the object of an evil spirit's attack, and it deranged him. He went mad, he went insane. And this is a man of whom it is said that God had touched his heart. This is a man of whom it is said that the Lord gave him another heart, a man who was regenerate by the Spirit of God; and yet you see this progressive disintegration. Now, this would be a very interesting case history and study in itself, to go through the several chapters of 1 Samuel and see the progressive breaking up of this man's mind and the intrusion of insanity into his whole being. And let us not dismiss this story as a primitive and naive attempt to describe something which of course, as they say, we would not call demon-influence today. This is something that the devil did, and does, and can do to people.

I referred in a earlier chapter to a letter written by Dr. Ken Irvine years ago about a strange experience through which he passed in the mission field, in which he felt pressures so great upon his mind, that he really began to feel, doctor as he was, that he was going insane. And after he had passed through this, he recognised that it was a demonic power attacking his mind. In this connection it is, in my view, beside the point to say that people who have such experiences may be constitutionally prone to mental disorder. Some may be—I do not know—some not. But the devil can attack sane and balanced minds too, and, if unchecked and undetected and unexposed, can wreck them. This is a factor in Christian experience. Sometimes Christians land in mental hospitals. Please be clear about what I am saying. I am not saying that all mental disorder is the work of the devil, in this direct sense. But some of it may be. And this is the point.

I do not know whether the reference that Paul makes in the opening verses of 2 Corinthians is to something of this nature or not, where he speaks of being pressed out of measure, above strength, insomuch that he despaired even of life. And he had the sentence of death in himself. But it may very well be. And I am sure that Paul was no stranger to these attacks. There was a point also in this same Epistle, chapter 7, where he said, 'Our flesh had no rest, but we were troubled on every side; without were fightings, within were fears'! What does that bear testimony to? The ordinary run of Christian experience, or something of a deep intensity? This, then, is the kind of thing that can happen. Once again, as I have had to say before, you may not know what I am talking about. But I am very sure that there are some who will read this who do know what I am talking about, and who may have experienced this very thing, the attack on the mind.

There is another area, however, in which the New Testament speaks of the devil as having an influence on the mind, and that is in the realm of wrong thinking, and particularly heresy. Paul speaks in 1 Timothy 4 of 'seducing spirits' and 'doctrines of devils', and in another place of 'strong delusions' and 'men believing lies'. No-one who has had experience of people deluded by heretical teaching could doubt that there is something demonic about the intransigence and the fanaticism with which they hold to, and propagate, their beliefs. And this is never an area in which we can assume as a matter of course that we are safe and will be unaffected. It is certainly not for nothing that Jesus once said, 'Take heed what ye hear. Many shall come in My name and shall deceive many.' This is an attack on the mind, not in relation to insanity, but to leading men completely and utterly astray. And in all conscience, there is so much wrong thinking today, not merely in the spiritual realm, or in the scriptural realm, but in realms which we would not normally associate with the Scripture or with heresy, but which are just as dangerous and just as devilish and disastrous for the lives of men.

Think, for example, of the techniques of brainwashing that are employed in some parts of the world today, in communist China, for example. When one reads some of the accounts of the brainwashing of believers in China it makes one's hair stand on end, and it forces the question, 'How would I possibly stand up to this?' Could we stand up to this? You may have read Geoffrey Bull's account of his three years and two months in Communist imprisonment in Chungking, when he was so thoroughly brain-washed. He does not say this in his book, but he later told one of his colleagues that, for six months and more after he came out of prison in Chungking, he could not even say the Lord's Prayer with any meaning, his mind was so bludgeoned and dazed and unfeeling. Something had been done to him. The attack on the mind.

We have heard about the brain-washing of the American crew of the Pueblo by the Koreans. This was an attack on their mind, with a view to changing people's personalities. Do you remember the stir there was a few years ago when William Sargent produced his book, *Battle for the Mind*, and the strictures it passed on some aspects of evangelistic method in the church—not without justification. These are the realms in which real issues are involved today. Do you remember, in the first chapter of Daniel, Nebuchadnezzar's determination to get the youth of his generation and brain-wash them, condition them, and shape them into something that he wanted. This is something that is absolutely topical today. There are powers in our country at the present time that are conditioning a whole generation in their thinking. It is commonplace to speak, for example, of the whole industry that has emerged and been created by ruthless and unscrupulous people to manipulate the young generation who have more money than ever any young generation has had. There is a field of exploitation there, and the whole of our

modern generation is exploited by business interests
—pop music, the record industry; there are millions
being made in this, because there is very skilful and
very ruthless brain-washing and conditioning of
people's mental attitudes. The attack on the mind.

There is a good deal written, for example, about
advertising, especially subliminal advertising, the
impact upon the unconscious. We could very truly
call this generation the manipulated generation. The
fact of the matter is, attacks on the mind are wide-
spread. Commercial interests, cultural interests—
look at the enormous impact that television viewing
is having upon the thinking of the country. Did you
know that Great Britain has the reputation in Europe
of being the dirtiest minded people in the world today? That is what they say about Great Britain
abroad. But the British people do not know it. They
have been got at. Their minds are being manipulated.
This is something terribly real and terribly dangerous. And all these things are the impact of wrong
thinking. As Christian people we need to be aware of
these trends.

As responsible people we have a duty to read, we
have a duty to allow good and right reading to influence our minds in a right and Christian way. Well,
read *The Screwtape Letters* and its sequel, *Screwtape
proposes a toast*, by C. S. Lewis. Read some of Lewis's
Essays on this very subject, and learn how the thinking of people in this country is being corrupted
silently, unconsciously.

I mentioned Sargent and his *Battle for the Mind*.
Dr. Martyn Lloyd Jones wrote a pamphlet in answer

to the thesis of that book, called *Conversations, Psychological or Spiritual?* That is something that people should read. And remember what Paul says—'The god of this world hath blinded the minds of them that believe not.' Well, if the god of this world can blind the minds of them that believe not, is it not feasible that he should be able also to condition the minds of those that do believe? That is what Paul is getting at. The battle for the mind. This is going on all the time. Our minds are being contested for, whether we will or not, whatever we read or do not read. Even if our minds are simply captured by the advertising hoarding, we are not our own, we are not free people. We are captured. Then there is the attack on the mind which paralyses thought, and causes the abdication of the mind to either emotion or unreason. Some of you who are *au fait* with this kind of thinking will know that there is a cult of the absurd, a very fashionable cult in literature at the present time, and in theatre. 'Be not mindless,' says the apostle, 'but understanding what the will of the Lord is.'

All this variety of attack is explained in terms of the fact that the mind has such an important, God-given function in the Christian life. Impair or damage it, reduce its capacity, and a great victory has been won by the evil one. Now what I have said will give some indication of the possibility of attack and the wide field in which attack may be expected. These are only some of the issues, not by any means all of them, that mirror this situation.

Now, Paul says, take the helmet of salvation, a helmet to protect our minds and preserve clear vision. And in view of what I have just said, this assumes an enormous importance—a helmet to protect our minds and to preserve clear vision, as we look out upon the world. And as I said at the beginning of this chapter, a mind constantly pre-occupied with thoughts of our great salvation is a mind kept safe from the assaults of the enemy. Yes, you say, that is simple and clear enough, and is the answer as simple as that? Well, you know, that is not a simple thing, for all the profundity of eternity is in it, as I want to explain in a moment. But in point of fact this is precisely where an attack is so often made on our thinking. For so often as believers we think we are thinking about God's great salvation, when in fact we are doing nothing of the kind. What we are doing is that we are being pre-occupied with our own spiritual states, with our spiritual condition, with our spiritual attitudes. We are being subjective, we are being introspective, and sometimes morbidly so.

This is not always or even, I suspect, often perceived by Christian people. They deem themselves to be taken up with spiritual things, with the Word and with prayer. But, all the time, the truth is they are simply taken up with themselves. Some people, some Christians, really never manage to escape from themselves. Their whole spiritual existence is geared to their own spiritual state. They are not thinking about God's great salvation. They are thinking of their experience of God's great salvation; they are turned inwards. They are ingrown in the soul. This is precisely why so many people make heavy weather of Christian life. They are pre-occupied; they are eternally probing inside their spiritual states. Do you know the lines of a very lovely evening hymn, 'The duteous day now closes'? One of the verses runs like this :

> *Now all the heavenly splendour*
> *Breaks forth in starlight tender*
> *From myriad worlds unknown;*
> *And man the marvel seeing,*
> *Forgets his selfish being,*
> *For joy of beauty not his own.*

Now, safety and salvation for some people, victory for some people, lies just here, 'Forgetting their selfish being', their spiritual selfish being, their Christian selfish being; because, spiritual self though it be, it is pre-occupied, and they need to die to their pre-occupation with themselves and their spiritual states. Pre-occupation with Christ must replace pre-occupation with holiness and with themselves. Poking about in the recesses of our minds and our hearts, psycho-analysing ourselves and psychoanalysing one another, is a luxury that we simply cannot afford in the Christian battle, if we are to keep our minds intact. It is a most unhealthy thing, Repeatedly we have to deal with people whose main and major problem lies just here. They are too pre-occupied with their spiritual states; they never let be. They need nothing so much as a breath of fresh air blowing through their experience, blowing away these unhealthy, morbid, introspective, inlooking thoughts. Look up, look up, says God.

By way of contrast, look at the experience of John the apostle on the Isle of Patmos. What was it that came to him, and became his helmet in that time of need? It was simply the consciousness of Christ; the bigness, the majesty, the magnitude of Christ. 'I am He that liveth and was dead, and behold I am alive for evermore.' 'The voice as the sound of many waters.' 'Worthy is the lamb that was slain.' These are the categories, you see—solid objective categories. Now I know that there is a subjective part to the spiritual life. But I am speaking about those that have forgotten all about the objective category. And objective thinking must become a habit with us, far more than it often is; and the objective truths and reality and glory of the gospel must become the substitute for the natural, merely natural, categories of our mortal lives. In this sense we must live a borrowed life, drawing constantly on the givenness of the Christian revelation in Christ. Here is a good test. In any hymn book, you have, in the main, two different kinds of hymns. There are those hymns which display the glory and the greatness of God and of His Son Jesus Christ, and speak of His mighty work in the cross and in His victory in the resurrection. There are those hymns, on the other hand, that are experimental, that is to say, they are speaking of what I feel and what I experience, my spiritual states. Now, as I say, both objective and subjective have their place in the Christian life. But when the subjective usurps the place of the objective and takes over, so to speak, in such a way that our favourite hymns are those that speak of longings for fullness and blessing, then something has gone wrong in our spiritual life. We are pre-occupied; and this is one of the great dangers of any holiness movement, that it simply concentrates attention upon this. Now it is a question of balance, I know. But think of the great Reformation hymns. There is no lack of subjectivism there. 'Ein Feste Burg', Luther's great hymn, 'A safe stronghold, our God is still', speaks of his experience, but the whole emphasis there is outward and upward, upon God. He is the great circumstance—not our feelings, not our longings, not our desires, not our yearnings. You see my point? Wrong thinking here spells defeat for the Christian life. This, simply, is the reason why some believers never get out of the bit in their spiritual lives; they are too pre-occupied, they are too taken up with themselves. They have got to die to this pre-occupation and fix their eyes upon Christ.

What this means in practical terms is this. Let me try to illustrate it. Each day must see us, at its outset, pushing back over the frontiers of our minds all the natural thoughts, the natural considerations, the natural attitudes, that are part and parcel of natural life, and, indeed, of spiritual life, and allowing the new life to possess. 'Whatsoever things are true, whatsoever things are honest, whatsoever things are just, whatsoever things are pure, whatsoever things are lovely, whatsoever things are of good report . . . think on these things.' This is a practical exercise. You are going to be faced tomorrow morning with two possibilities: either with the prospect of thinking and mulling over your own spiritual states, and how dissatisfied you are—and this may be perfectly true—or you may by the grace of God put on a helmet and let your mind be possessed by the powers of the world to come, and instead of thinking about your longings and your hunger and your yearnings, you will think of Christ in His majesty and His glory; and that will do something to you, because that kind of thinking is like no other kind of thinking. It is radio-active in the spiritual sense. It will create a new climate in your mind. You see my point? I am putting it starkly, but this sums up the whole issue. If we were honest and sat down to examine the content of our prayer life, for example, how much of it would we find to have been pre-occupied with things relating to 'me'—'my spiritual state', 'my spiritual progress', 'my spiritual hunger', 'my spiritual yearnings', 'my spiritual longings', 'my spiritual—'? Some people never escape from themselves; they are in bondage to their own spiritual life. And it is hardly surprising, as someone once said to me, that such people should look very droopy Christians. They deserve to be droopy! This whole process is subject to the law of diminishing returns. You have to probe more and more, to get less and less satisfaction. What a tangle some folk get into in their spiritual lives!

Paul says. 'Put on your helmet, the helmet of salvation.' Think of your great salvation. Think of the glory and wonder of the forgiveness of God. Think of the mystery of the reconciling love of God, grappling with the mass of the world's sin on the cross of Calvary, crushing it, breaking it. 'And man the marvel seeing, forgets his selfish being, for joy of beauty not his own.' Oh, the relief just to stop thinking about ourselves for a while! Think of the greatness of the mystery of regeneration. Think of our position in Christ. Think of what God has made us. Think of the wonder of that term, 'If any man be in Christ, he is a new creation.' Think of it. A new creation! And think of what Paul says of the believer as being married to One who has been raised from the dead. That is some marriage! Never a dull moment there! Resurrection dynamic, and we are linked to it. Think of that! And think of the wonder of being called 'sons and daughters of God'. 'Behold what manner of love the Father hath bestowed upon us that we should be called the sons of God.' Think of what we shall be. That is where the hope of salvation comes in. You see, the helmet protects the eyes as well as the head, and keeps our sights clear. And so we look ahead. And as we know, everywhere in the New Testament Scriptures the blessed hope is held out as an incentive to steadfastness and holiness of living. The great resurrection chapter, 1 Corinthians 15, ends up, 'Therefore, my beloved brethren, be ye steadfast, unmoveable, always abounding in the work of the Lord.' You see the pattern? Put on your helmet, and you will stand firm. You know the words of the hymn:

> The eternal glories gleam afar,
> To nerve my faint endeavour;
> So now to watch, to work, to war,
> And then to rest forever.

'The eternal glories gleam afar . . .' Catch a sight of what you shall be. God's ultimate purpose for your life. That will steady you. That will keep your mind. That will protect your eyes. It will do something to you. And whatever else you may say about the New Testament writers, this much is true: they lived life in this world with a due sense of responsibility, but it is easy to see that their loyalties were elsewhere. They were pilgrims and strangers upon the earth. They were sojourners; they were lodgers here. Let no-one think that is a sentimental, escapist doctrine. It is the most practical thing in the world, rightly understood. My helmet keeps my eyes clear, keeps my vision clear, so that I can see this. And as long as my eyes are on this, all is going to be well. Nebuchadnezzar can brain-wash me, but I'll see something that he has not seen, and all will be well. Take the helmet of salvation, and may God bless you.

7

THE SWORD OF THE SPIRIT

WITH THIS piece of the Christian armour we pass from defence to attack. The sword is an attacking instrument and weapon, and a little thought will make it plain that there is necessarily a two-fold implication in this. First of all, attack as the best form of defence, that is to say hitting back at the enemy when he has been attacking us in the ways we have been thinking about in the past chapters; and secondly, attack in the context of Christian service generally, in preaching, in evangelism, in testimony and witness, and so on. And this is the way in which we are going to look at the subject in this chapter.

But first of all a word or two, by way of introduction, on the terms that Paul uses here. You will probably remember that in earlier chapters about the other parts of the armour we have interpreted the phrases simply. For example, the helmet of salvation we have taken to mean the helmet which is salvation, and that makes good sense; and shield of faith, the shield which is faith. But I do not think you can do that with this phrase here: 'the sword of the Spirit which is the word of God'. It cannot mean the sword which is the Spirit because it is not the Spirit that is the sword; it is the word of God that is the

sword. And it is the Spirit that uses it. Now Paul
means something more here than simply to take a
spiritual sword which is the word of God, although
of course the word of God is a spiritual sword, and
this is probably what Paul means in the passage in 2
Corinthians 10, for example, where he says, 'The
weapons of our warfare are not carnal, but mighty
through God to the pulling down of strongholds.' Not
carnal but spiritual weapons. But he does not mean
quite that here. It is the Holy Spirit Himself who is
meant and referred to, and this therefore must mean
that it is the Holy Spirit in us that uses the sword
against the enemy. Now think that one over for a
moment. It is the Holy Spirit in us who uses the
sword against the enemy. And the Holy Spirit has
freedom to work in us only as He fills and controls us.
So that one necessary prerequisite for success in wag-
ing the spiritual warfare is to have put our lives at
the entire disposal, and into the entire control, of the
Spirit of God. A Spirit-filled man, a Spirit-controlled
man, is the only one likely to make much of a show-
ing against the powers of darkness. No other wielding the word of God is likely to make much headway
or find much success. The word is the Spirit's sword
and, when he uses it, it is always with effect. The
Spirit working in us—and this, of course, links up
with the passage in Ephesians 5 where Paul insists
that we be filled with the Spirit. This is the point.
You cannot wield the sword of the Spirit which is the
word of God unless in fact you are filled with the
Spirit.

Well now, let us think of the first consideration:

attack as the best form of defence. The first and introductory thing that we must say here is that we must
recognise just how trusty and reliable is the blade
which is put into our hands. We read in Hebrews 4,
'The word of God is living, and powerful, and
sharper than any two-edged sword, piercing even to
the dividing asunder of soul and spirit, and of the
joints and marrow, and is a discerner of the thoughts
and intents of the heart.' And it is not our wielding of
it, but its own inherent, living power in our hands,
that proves dynamic. It is not something that we do.
As Luther says, 'With force of arms we nothing can.'
It is the sword itself. Perhaps I can put it like this :
when you take the sword of the Spirit which is the
word of God into your hand it is not you who wave
it; it is the sword that waves your hand. That is the
point, if we can think of such a gloriously mixed-up
metaphor. That is the power and dynamic. It is
almost as if it takes over and we are not controlling it
but it is controlling us. That is the first thing we have
to remember, to recognise. A good part of our failure
in the Christian life is simply a failure to recognise
the potency of this instrument that is in our hands.

And secondly, the Greek for 'word of God' here is
not the usual word that we have in the New Testament, *logos*, but the word *rema*, and one commentator says that in almost every instance in which this
is used for the 'word of God' it means a definite divine
utterance. Now I think this is of real significance,
because it means that the sword that we are thinking
of is not so much the Scriptures in general—of course
it will include that, it speaks of that—but the specific

word that God gives us in specific and particular cases
of need. That is the sword. Now this is something
tremendously practical. You remember what Jesus
said to His disciples when He sent them forth:
Matthew 10. 19, 'When they deliver you up, take no
thought how or what ye shall speak: for it shall be
given you in that same hour what ye shall speak.'
That is to say, God places a sword in your hand at
the strategic moment and He gives you the word to
speak. Now read that into the 'armour' passage, and
think of it in terms of God putting a weapon into our
hands at the crucial moment.

Now a corollary to that is this. That word, that
weapon, is given us by the Spirit in His function of
bringing to our remembrance the word that we have
read and stored and hid in our hearts. And it is never
apart from this. When the Spirit of God is regnant in
our hearts, He makes us proficient in the Word, and
this is where the great discipline of regular and systematic study of the Scriptures comes in, storing it up
in our hearts. 'They word have I hid in my heart, that
I might not sin against thee.' A life steeped in the
Scriptures. That does not mean that we are necessarily able to turn up chapter and verse. Some people
have very good memories. I used to be able to do
that without any difficulty, but now that I'm growing
older my memory is not the same as it was! But that
is not the point. If God's Word is hid in our hearts,
then the Spirit has a reserve on which to call, and
the Spirit, so to speak, goes into our hearts and says,
'Now what will we use for this crisis? That word',
and he pulls it out. Have you not had that experi-

ence? In a moment of crisis, there comes a word right home to you, out of the blue, so to speak. But it is not out of the blue; it is out of your heart where the Word has been stored, perhaps years back. The word comes, and it is placed in your hands and it is a sword, and you thrash the power of the enemy with it. This is why it is so tremendously important to be praying that God will enable us to store in our hearts the word that we hear and read, against the day of trouble. In any particular situation when the word is expounded and taught, it may not be speaking to your present need, although it will surely speak to some present needs. But even though it is not for your present need, store it up. Lay it by, against the day of need. What I said about the devil's attack on the mind may not have been everybody's problem. You may not have needed that word, but you do not know when you will need it. But if it has been stored up in your heart then the Spirit will draw it out at the strategic moment, and make use of it, and put it in your hand.

Our Lord's own example here is relevant in His warfare with the enemy, in the wilderness, in the time of temptation. Thrice He was given a word from the Book of Deuteronomy, which proved effective in routing the enemy. 'It is written, Man shall not live by bread alone.' 'It is written, Thou shalt not tempt the Lord thy God.' 'It is written, Thou shalt worship the Lord thy God, and him only shalt thou serve.' These words were given to the Lord by the Spirit. He had just been filled and anointed by the Spirit at His baptism. But they were not given Him out of the blue. He had been trained in the Scriptures from a child. He had stored up the word of God in His heart, and it was from a heart filled with the word of God that the Spirit drew this precious armoury. You see my point? From His remembrance and recollection of the Scriptures in which he had been nurtured and nourished the Spirit of God took this. Oh, it is a great thought! Stock up; lay in supplies against the evil day—this is the thing. It is some years ago now since Billy Graham impressed so many people when he told a public gathering that he was encouraging his children to memorise big portions of the Scriptures against a possible time when oppression would be the order of the day for the Christian church, and there would be no Bibles and no freedom to preach, no freedom to hear the Word. Well, there you are: stock up against the evil day.

In the light of this, let us look at the use of the sword to defend us against the various attacks that we have already been studying. We began with the loins girt about with truth, and we stressed that the attack here was along the line of doubting God's word. 'Yea, hath God said?'—this is how Satan attacked Adam and Eve in the garden. 'Yea, hath God said?'—plunging an arrow of doubt into our first parents. And this was exactly the line that Satan took with our Lord in the wilderness. God had just declared from heaven, 'This is my beloved Son, in whom I am well pleased', and what does Satan come along and say? 'If thou be the Son of God . . .' You see? 'Do you really believe that? This is my beloved Son? It was just an imagination, Jesus. If thou be the Son of

God, command that these stones be made bread.' This can often be a very real and devastating attack, doubt of God's word, the secret loosening of convictions in the hearts of men. Now, how to counter it ? With the sword of the Spirit, the word of God. And we must learn to set over against that kind of attack, the Scripture's testimony to itself concerning its authority and its inspiration.

It is as practical as this. We come to a point, we perhaps read the writings of some clever men who make it sound very plausible and very convincing that of course the Bible cannot really be inerrant, it cannot really be in all parts absolutely, entirely inspired, and so on. These attacks can be very plausible and we must learn over against them to set the Scripture's testimony to itself : 'All Scripture is God-breathed.' 'Holy men spake as they were moved by the Holy Ghost.' And the objective reality of that testimony—use that as a sword against this. That is the way to deal with it. It is written ! Let these mighty words assail the tempter. That word in 2 Timothy 3. 16, 'All Scripture is given by inspiration of God, and is profitable', is an anvil, if I can mix the metaphors again, that has worn out many of the devil's hammers, and it is a sword that we can use to assail the enemy, to defend ourselves by attacking him. Slash that word into him, and let the bare word of God do the work, remembering what I said at the beginning, that God's word is living. That is where to go, the Scripture's testimony to itself. This is the special word that God gives.

Then the breastplate of righteousness; and we

stressed that here there was the attack on our standing in grace and the doubts that come about one's salvation. How do we counter-attack when we are doubting our salvation? Well, we take the sword, that is to say, the special words in the Scripture about assurance of salvation. You know the old saying. 'The shed blood makes us safe, the written word makes us sure'; that is a good working formula. Take particular words that God has given to us to rest upon. 'These things have I written unto you,' says John, 'that ye may know that ye have eternal life.' This is one of the functions of the reading of the Scriptures, that we may know that we have eternal life. Let me give you an instance of this. I remember at the end of the last war, when I was still in the Forces, stationed in Inverness, I was passing through a time of real spiritual difficulty and particularly I was deeply exercised about my call to the ministry. Before I was called up I had committed myself to the work of the ministry, and during these war years I was very severely sifted in one way or another, and the whole situation was in the melting pot. It was a time of very severe doubt about my whole future. I was due to be demobilised fairly soon, and I did not know what to do, and what was bothering me was this—the awful fear lest going into the ministry was just something that I had taken into my own mind, some notion of my own, some emotional extravaganza that had no relation to a real call from God. And I remember sitting on the banks of the River Ness in the summer of 1945 in absolute misery. I was gazing across the water of the river and inwardly crying to God to make me sure. And my eyes fell upon my New Testament which was lying opened on my knee. And the first thing my eyes saw was this: the verse which reads, 'Ye have not chosen me, but I have chosen you, and ordained you, that ye should go and bring forth fruit, and that your fruit should remain.' There is not a verse in the whole Bible that could have answered my specific need as that verse did that day. I could have danced on the banks of the Ness when that word came to me. That was the sword that God had put in my hand with which to dismiss the attack of the enemy. You see? This is the way. He gives us the word, literally drops it in our lap, and says, 'Now pick it up and use it against the devil.' That was a great experience for me. I was doubting and wondering whether in fact I had been doing the choosing and that it was just my own notion. 'No,' said Christ, 'You have not chosen me; I have chosen you.'

Then, feet shod with the preparation of the gospel of peace. The attack here is on our stand, our standing firm, and this is the attempt to discourage us, to make us give up, to make us flee. Here, in particular, it is a matter of resting upon the special words from God, and using them and setting them over against the most determined attempts of Satan to down us. We find a remarkable instance of this in Isaiah 49. Israel is complaining in deep discouragement that God has forgotten her, and God comes and says, 'Can a woman forget her sucking child, that she should not have compassion on the son of her womb? Yea, they may forget, yet will I not forget thee. Behold, I have graven thee upon the palms of my hands.' That is a sword with which to dispel the attacks of discouragement. Are you discouraged? Do you feel like giving up? I pray God that he will put a sword into your hand that will enable you to drive off the attacks. Let me tell you about Samuel Chadwick the Methodist saint of God who, saint though he was, was a man of like passions as we are and had his moments of discouragement like the rest of us. It was a Monday morning and he had a sense of desolation and failure upon his spirit. He came to a great friend of his and told him about this, told him of his discouragement about his services the previous day. He said, 'You know, man, I feel like a worm.' And his friend said 'Well, Samuel, here is God's word to a worm. Listen. "Fear not, thou worm Jacob . . . I will help thee." ' Are you feeling like a worm? Well, turn to Isaiah 41. 14–18. That is for you. 'Fear not, thou worm Jacob . . . I will help thee.'

Then, the fiery darts of the wicked. Here, faith must rest on the bare word of God and be strengthened by that word. We spoke in connection with the fiery darts of darkness and doubt, and the overwhelming temptations that sometimes sweep in upon the spirit. We must just rest upon God's word. 'Fear not: for I have redeemed thee, I have called thee by thy name; thou art mine. When thou passest through the waters, I will be with thee; and through the rivers, they shall not overflow thee.' That is the word: wield it, slash the enemy with it. He cannot stand that kind of verse.

The attacks on the mind, the helmet of salvation. Over against them all—this confusion, this nightmarish quality, this bombardment of the mind—we must set the word of God in its sanity, in its balance, its fresh air, its truth. Have you ever felt as if you were living through a nightmare? This is the feeling I sometimes get when I read modern literature and perhaps, most of all, the existentialist literature, Sartre, Camus, and these others. When you read these books, you feel as if you are going mad. It is a world that is so frightening, so meaningless. And often existence is like that. People feel the meaningless of everything. Now these are the evil one's attacks on the mind, and what we need to offset that is the absolute sanity of the word of God. This is the only sword that will keep us in the midst of such meaninglessness.

There is a book entitled *The Mark of Cain* (Paternoster Press, 1967) which could well be read with profit in relation to this, because it deals with this meaninglessness in the modern world of literature and the arts. And we must believe in the power of the word of God to cut through it, to slice through it, its lies, its pretensions. And let us remember this, that the sword is not a weak thing: it is a two-edged weapon; it can slash and cut through this. We must remember, also, it is not always the first stroke of the sword that wins a fight. I think that sometimes believers forget this. They take the word of God and they use it as a sword and it does not work. They say, 'It does not work; it cannot be right.' But all they have done is to give one slash. And the enemy is not always defeated by one slash of the sword. You have to ply the sword. There has to be a lot of sword play

—right and left and centre! And we have to gain
the victory. 'This is the victory that overcometh the
world,' says John, 'even our faith.' You see? Attack
is the best method of defence.

But then there is the attack in the truest sense, in
service and witness, by which we carry the war into
the enemy's camp. Here again the first necessity is to
recognise that the word is a living thing with inherent
power. Listen to what the Psalmist says: 'Thy word
have I hid in my heart, that I might not sin against
thee.' Now, no inert word could do that. An ordinary
word hid in a man's heart could not do that. It is a
living thing. And because it is a living thing, it is
likely to have incalculable effect when taken up by
the Spirit in us. And if the lines are clear between us
and God, it will have this effect.

Look at Peter on the day of Pentecost. Peter's sermon was simply a gathering-together of texts from
the Old Testament, relating them to the historical
situation through which they had passed. 'This that
has happened in Jerusalem in these days,' he said, 'is
that which was prophesised of old time.' He went
through the prophetic Scriptures. He took the sword.
And what happened? It had the desired effect. His
hearers were pricked in their hearts. God's word was
like a sword that slashed through these very men who
crucified the Son of God, these very men, be it noted,
who had remained intransigent in face of all our
Lord's own teaching, who had remained consistently
opposed to Him, and who showed no sign during His
ministry of being changed. And this man, Peter, filled
with the Holy Ghost, took the sword, he laid about

him with it, and devastated them. The sword of the Spirit which is the word of God.

And do you recall what Paul says in Romans 7? 'When the commandment came, sin revived and I died.' My word, that was something! When the commandment came. When the sword of the word of God touched that man's life, it started something absolutely incalculable. What an attack that must have been! Or read through the Acts of the Apostles and see the apostolic use of the sword. The disciples went everywhere preaching the Word.

> *Like a mighty army*
> *Moves the Church of God;*
> *Brothers, we are treading*
> *Where the saints have trod.*

This is it, bearing the sword—in preaching, and in personal witness alike. It is never a question of one human mind against another. If it were so, how little hope there would be of ordinary folk like ourselves accomplishing anything in the work of the gospel. No, it is ordinary human minds, wielding a supernatural sword of power. And that is sufficient for any victory. I heard a while ago about an Admiral of the British Fleet who had been led to Jesus Christ in London by a teenage girl—led to Christ by a teenager in London, because she had a sword in her hand, and that sword did the mighty work.

Therefore, know your sword. Get to know it well and practise the use of it. Turn it on yourself first, to slay the evil things in your own heart. 'Wherewithal

shall a young man cleanse his way? by taking heed
thereto according to thy word.' Is there uncleanness
in your life? Slash it with the sword of God's word.
'Sanctify them through thy truth: thy word is truth'
—sanctification by the Word. 'Thy word have I hid
in my heart that I might not sin against thee'—the
keeping power of the word of God. There is nothing
that God's word cannot do. And having dealt with
ourselves, we turn to deal with others. Paul says, 'God
. . . hath made us able ministers of the new testament;
not of the letter, but of the Spirit: for the letter
killeth, but the spirit giveth life', and 'Where the
Spirit of the Lord is, there is liberty.' Take the sword
of the Spirit—and as I said before, the word 'take'
has the force of 'receiving'. It is something you
receive from the hand of Another. Receive the sword
of the Spirit which is the word of God.

The thing that has helped me most in this study is
the realisation that 'word' in the Greek means a
specific word—a specific utterance. It tells me that
in specific need, in particular situations, God is going
to give me the sword that will match it. Now you
have a particular occasion today. I do not know what
it is. You know it. And this is what God is saying:
'My child, in the hour that you need, it will be given
you.' Receive the sword of the Spirit, which is the
word of God.

8

ALL-PRAYER

SOME HAVE thought that the weapon of all-prayer is hardly to be considered as a piece of Christian armour in the same sense as the other parts—the helmet of salvation, the shield of faith, and so on. But surely when one thinks a little of the Christian warfare it becomes clear that this is in some ways the most important weapon of all, for it is the foundation of all the others. One of the great hymns says, 'Each piece put on with prayer.' And this is the emphasis here. Pray when you are girding your loins with the truth. Pray when you are putting on the breastplate of righteousness. Pray when you are putting on your feet the preparation of the gospel of peace. Pray when you are taking the shield of faith. Pray when you put on the helmet of salvation. Pray when you are wielding the sword of the Spirit. Otherwise none of them will work. If the Christian life is a battle—as Paul invites us to consider it here—and if we are soldiers, then it is of the utmost importance that we should have lines of communication established between ourselves and our great Captain. If communications break down, the battle will be in jeopardy, and may end in disorder and disaster for us. And our communication-line is prayer.

In this, as in so many aspects of Christian life, Christ is the great example. You will remember how often in the Gospels we see Him at prayer. Matthew represents Jesus as a king going forth into battle, conquering, and to conquer. And at every point, and especially at high moments of crisis in His life and ministry, we see the King at prayer. When Jesus was baptised, we see Him praying. We see Him in Mark's Gospel praying after works of healing, and before choosing the twelve. We see Him at prayer after great achievements, such as feeding the five thousand. We see Him at prayer when He was very busy, precisely the moments when we usually leave prayer out. We see Him in prayer at His transfiguration. We see Him in the upper room in prayer for His disciples. We see Him in prayer in Gethsemane, and He was praying on the cross. And in all this, He left us an example that we should follow in His steps.

Now, like the sword of the Spirit which is the word of God this weapon of all-prayer can be used both defensively and in attack, to defend ourselves and others from the enemy, and also to attack the enemy on our own behalf and on behalf of others. But even defensive prayer, in which we pray to God for protection for ourselves and for His work, and for His workers, is an attack on Satan, in that it foils Satan's designs on God's people, by setting at nought his purposes to harm them. Remember Jesus' own use of this weapon when He said to Simon Peter, 'Simon, Simon, Satan hath desired to have you, that he may sift you as wheat: but I have prayed for thee, that thy faith fail not.' That is the weapon of all-prayer. Christ made use of it to protect Peter against Satan. But I think the reference here, for all that, is principally to attacking prayer, rather than defensive, and for this reason: Paul adds in verse 19 the words, 'Pray for me, that utterance may be given unto me, that I may open my mouth boldly.' In other words, he gives here an instance of what he means, of prayer as an integral factor in the proclamation of the gospel.

There are three points that we have to note particularly here. The first is the word 'always'—praying always. This is something Paul echoes elsewhere. In 1 Thessalonians 5, for example, he says, 'Pray without ceasing', and this in turn is simply an echo of our Lord's own teaching in Luke 18, when He illustrated in the parable of the unjust judge that 'men ought always to pray, and not to faint'. Concerning that parable in Luke 18, early church commentators point out that it finds its significant meaning in relation to what has just gone before in the previous chapter, namely the descriptions of the sufferings and the distresses of the last days, and the birth pangs of the new creation. The idea is that since the fight of faith will increase in intensity and fierceness in the last days, only incessant, importunate prayer will keep us from fainting and going down in the battle. This is the point that Jesus is making. And He goes on to show them how men ought always to pray, and not to faint. And this is what Paul means here when he says, 'Stand therefore', 'that ye may be able to withstand in the evil day, and having done all, to stand'—

when the fierceness of the onslaught is past, to be found still standing and not having crumpled in the middle of it, men ought always to pray.

This word 'always' can hardly refer to stated times of prayer, in the sense of retiring into the secret place to pray. It must surely refer to another kind of prayer. It is true that Jesus taught by precept and example the duty and the necessity and the import-ance of times of prayer, and places of prayer, in which we draw aside and specifically commit our-selves to prayer. This much is not in question. But there is also such a thing as a spirit of prayer, and an attitude of prayer, and I think it is to this Paul must be referring here, because not otherwise could we be always praying. We have our work to do, we cannot always be in the secret place, and we may not neglect our necessary duties for the place of prayer. But there is a spirit of prayer, and an attitude of prayer, and when we are in that attitude we can be praying always. If this is so, what does it apply to, and what does it imply? Well, I think it implies this, that it is the quality of our lives, what we are, that will determine our prayer and our contact with God and our ability to draw on the divine resources. It has a moral reference, and it amounts to this: if we are right people, then we will pray always, and if we are not, we cannot and we will not; even if we were on our knees all day long, we would not pray as God means us to pray. It is not how we pray, and what we pray, but what we are when we pray, that is decisive. Our life is our prayer. And if our life is not right neither will our prayer be right, however earnestly we may stir ourselves in prayer. And this, of course, is the importance of the first part of the Epistle to the Ephesians, where Paul is so concerned that believers should enter into all their wealth in Christ and make it their own, because then they will be right.

Here is a believer who is living close to God, he has exposed his life to the discipline of the Word of God, he has let God's word slay all that is alien to the will of God in his life; in the most costly kind of way he has opened himself to the incoming of God's drastic surgery in the Word, and let God do a work in him, and he has responded, and been renewed, and transformed within. This work is ever deepening, and continuing—it challenges him at deeper and deeper levels, and he rises to the challenge, and meets it, He is, as we might say, a crucified man, moment by moment, day by day. Now that life, in practical terms, is a living sacrifice to God, holy and acceptable; and in that sense it is a constant prayer. God hears that life. Is not that a wonderful thought, that God hears a life? It speaks to God, and it speaks with God, and there is a blessed, intimate, unbroken fellowship with Him that moves His hand. I am persuaded that this is the secret of the prayer giants in the Scriptures, men who moved the world of God. It is what they were that really mattered. With Elijah on Mount Carmel, a simple sentence of prayer brought the fire down. It was not the simple sentence of prayer that brought the fire down really; it was the prayer that was ascending from his life all day long. It was what Elijah was that spoke to God in that way, and required the fire to come down. And so with Moses and so with Abraham.

This is what Paul means by 'praying always'. And if we are like that, we will be praying always; our life will be sending up signals every moment of the day to the living God. The moral energy of prayer derives from moral rectitude, which in turn comes through inward crucifixion, and, without this, prayer is an empty shell. It is a conformity to the mind of Christ. 'Let this mind be in you, which was also in Christ Jesus' (Phil. 2). And this means intimacy of fellowship with God. The men who have moved the world of God have always been like this. Praying always. We will never pray at all in this sense unless we are a certain type of person. This is why it is so much beside the point for people simply to decide, 'I will pray a bit more every day.' This is not the way. Praying a bit more every day, of course, has its place. We all ought to pray a bit more every day. But God is looking on the life, and it is a life that speaks, not a voice; what we are, not what we say. That is why prayer is really the end-product of the work of discipline in the soul by the Word and Spirit of God. If we open ourselves unreservedly to the discipline of God's word, that will make us into praying men and women. Praying always. That is the Christian warrior.

And then, secondly, Paul goes on to say, 'watching thereunto with all perseverance and all supplication for all saints.' Now this is really very striking, the more you think about it. One might have thought that when addressing the Ephesians on spiritual warfare,

Paul would have made a particular reference to their own battles, but he does not. Paul's mind is on something different. His mind, in fact, is on outward, objective prayer, not inward, subjective prayer. And what that means is this. It means that although it is our battle, naturally, that is our personal concern, the weapon of all-prayer is not to be used exclusively or even primarily for our personal battle. Once again, this seems to me to bear out our Lord's own teaching on the subject of prayer. In the Lord's Prayer, for example, you will recall how He said, 'When ye pray, say,

> *Our Father which art in heaven,*
> *Hallowed be thy name.*
> *Thy kingdom come.*
> *Thy will be done, in earth as it is in heaven.'*

That is to say, our prayer, first of all and primarily, is to be entirely taken up with the things of God, with the honour and glory of His great name and the coming of His kingdom; and only then, when that divine order is established, personal needs:

> *'Give us this day our daily bread.*
> *Forgive us our debts.*
> *Lead us not into temptation.'*

This is an entirely safe and healthy order. And it does cut across merely natural instinct and inclination, for in fact the tendency, in time of testing, is that we do become pre-occupied with our own particular problem, or battle, or temptation, or struggle. But Paul seems to indicate here, 'Do not concentrate your prayer upon that; pray not for yourself, but for all saints'. And I think I can understand why Paul gives us this emphasis. I think I can hear him say, 'Self pre-occupying prayer leads to morbidity.' Often the worst thing we can do about our temptations is to pray about them, because praying about them simply focuses our attention upon them, and one never gets away from them at all. One gets bogged down with them. This is subject to the law of diminishing returns. The more we pray inwardly, in an inward direction, the less help we get from our prayers, and soon we are in a morass of depression. Paul's advice here is, 'Relate your personal battle to *the* battle. Strike a blow for the larger cause in your prayer. Look at the main strategy of God, not merely at the one infinitesimal part that is your problem.' Now in this connection let me quote from Arthur Hugh Clough's hymn—

> *Say not, The struggle nought availeth;*
> *The labour and the wounds are vain;*
> *The enemy faints not our faileth,*
> *And as things have been they remain.*
>
> *If hopes were dupes, fears may be liars:*
> *It may be, in yon smoke concealed,*
> *Your comrades chase even now the fliers,*
> *And, but for you, possess the field.*

But we are moaning about our failure, moaning about our own problems!

For while the tired waves, vainly breaking,
Seem here no painful inch to gain,
Far back, through creeks and inlets making,
Comes, silent, flooding in, the main.

What a glorious simile that is! Have you got it? 'For while the tired waves, vainly breaking, seem here no painful inch to gain'—you see, that is one way of looking at our problem, our battle—we are battling on, we are not getting out of the bit, and we are getting discouraged, and we say, What is the use? That is what we get for praying for ourselves.

Far back through creeks and inlets making,
Comes silent, flooding in, the main.
And not by eastern windows only,
When daylight comes, comes in the light,
In front, the sun climbs slow, how slowly,
But westward, look! the land is bright.

A great hymn. Great words. Read it; study it well. You have got the two ideas here: one's discouragement with the inches only of advance that we are making, and, on the other hand, the grand strategy of which our little concern is just one infinitesimal part. Paul's advice is, 'Relate your battle to *the* battle, strike the blow for the larger cause, look at the main strategy, not merely at the one little part of it that is your problem.'

Also, says Paul, relate your little battle to the main battle, in the sense of trying to understand yours in relation to it. Ask yourself this question, Why am I under attack? What relation does this attack upon you, whether temptation or anything else, bear to the overall strategy of God? Paul says, these little battles can all be related to the larger work and our part in it. And we have to pray therefore for the larger work, the main strategy, that it may go forward and be fulfilled. And when it goes forward and is fulfilled, we will be carried forward with it, and we will find our little problem dealt with in the movement; in the larger victory, we will be victorious too. Let me try to illustrate this.

God purposes a work of grace in a particular situation, it may be in a congregational situation, and He lays His plans and He begins to work. God is never in a hurry, and the great movements of God's Spirit in past history in Scotland, for example, have had long antecedents. Very well, He has a purpose of grace, and He lays plans, and Satan sets out to frustrate them. That is what is going on behind the scenes. Now in the concrete situation what we see is this: unaccountably, various people come under pressure in different ways. One fine believer begins to be assailed with the most awful temptations, and he is in deep water right away. Another believer has a major crisis in the home; this one here is passing through the deep waters of doubt and difficulty; that one there is being gripped unaccountably by a black discouragement. There is one believer who seems to begin to slack off in his Christian committal; and this believer is laid suddenly aside in sickness. And so on. Now these on the surface bear absolutely no relation to one another. But this is how the enemy works in a fellowship. At first they do not know this; they are not aware of the purpose of grace to come. They are simply conscious of their own personal problem and they are crying to God about it: 'O God, raise me from this sick bed. O God, this problem in my home; deal with it.' Now, says Paul, look up to the wider horizons. Ask yourself, Why is this happening to me? This is where the advantage of real fellowship comes in, because fellowship means sharing. It is certainly not the will of God that in time of trouble we should lock up our problems in our own hearts and share them with nobody. What is fellowship for, if it is not for sharing the burdens? 'Bear ye one another's burdens and so fulfil the law of Christ,' Paul says.

And when they are shared, it is then that there is the possibility of people putting two and two together. And they say, 'So and so is under fire just now, and so is he, and so is she.' And they begin to say 'Why are all these things happening?' Well, this is the enemy's strategy, and Paul says, 'Ask these questions and see that they are all in relation to the wider strategy of God; and pray for all saints, get into gear for the main battle. Play your part in that, let that victory be won and your own victory will come with it.' That, it seems to me, is the message that Paul is trying to get over to us here, and I think it is an immensely important one. Play your part in the big battle; in a sense, never mind your own one. Get into gear for the big one, remember you are a soldier, and in the stress of battle even wounded soldiers go on and carry on, not heeding the wounds. 'Play your part in that', says Paul, 'for all saints.

Let that victory be won and your own victory will come with it.' That is a great way to think and a great way to live. Let us take this as a practical proposition. Next time you are under pressure, my dear friend, relate it to the work of the fellowship. We are a unit; God has called us together. He has unified us into a working, fighting force. No attack comes to you personally, out of relation to anything else. It is all in relation to what we are committed to. See it all in that respect, and pray for the larger work. When the work of our church or fellowship goes forward like that, we will all go forward with it. We will be carried forward in the blessed surge of the Spirit's grace and power. Pray for that victory, and your own victory will be coming with it. Remember what we are told in the book of Job at the end of that wonderful story. 'The Lord turned the captivity of Job when he prayed for his friends.' 'For all saints.'

Thirdly, Paul says, 'And for me', and here we see particularly that the idea of attack is in Paul's mind. 'Pray,' he says, 'for me, that utterance may be given me.' And this is a particular instance and a particular example of his thesis. Focus your prayer here, he says, and this will give the gospel word power to make inroads into the kingdom of darkness, and this in turn will help you. Do you see the pattern? Paul is gently but firmly lifting the Ephesians' minds from their own woes. He says, 'Come now; I know you have problems; I know it is hard for you, but relate this to the bigger issue. Look, here is the spearhead; I am out there preaching the gospel.' He wrote this from Corinth. And he was up against it in Corinth.

'Pray for me,' he said, 'that utterance may be given me, that I may open my mouth boldly and make known the mystery of the gospel.' Remember that other word in 2 Thessalonians where Paul said, 'Finally, brethren, pray for us, that the word of the Lord may have free course, and be glorified ... and that we may be delivered from unreasonable and wicked men: for all men have not faith.' What did Paul mean by that? Well, there is so much there, if you will allow me to depart from Ephesians to this word which is an explanation of what he is saying here. 'Pray for us, that the word of the Lord may have free course.' That word in the Greek literally means 'that the word of God may run', and what he is asking for is for the kind of prayer that will set the gospel word like a fire blazing through the place. We sometimes speak of something spreading like a prairie fire. That is Paul's idea here. 'I want prayer that the word may have free course, that it might run like that.'

And there is this interesting phrase, 'that we may be delivered from unreasonable and wicked men, for all men have not faith'. 'All men have not faith' has more to it than we read on the surface. It is a statement of the obvious to say that all men have not faith. What he really means is, 'All men have not faith here who should have faith.' And he was experiencing difficulty and hindrance and frustration in the work of the gospel from the very people who should have been right behind him, the very people whom one would expect to have faith. Who is he referring to? The Jews, who, by tradition, by background and training, had everything in their favour. These were the very men that should have responded to Jesus Christ and the gospel. But they were the ones who were most bitterly opposed.

This was the thing that always mystified the apostle Paul. He could never understand this, that these people, the covenant, privileged people, whose were the prophets, who had the covenants and the promises turned their backs. 'All men have not faith,' he said. 'I am faced with this unaccountable opposition; therefore pray for me, brethren, that the sharp thrust of the sword of God's Spirit, which is the word of God, might break into that opposition.' The word 'unreasonable' here in the Greek literally means 'out of place'. These men were 'out of place' and this is where the deepest opposition often comes from; people who should have been in place, but were out of place; people who should have responded, who had everything to make them respond, but who bitterly opposed the gospel. And Paul says, 'Pray for us, that the word of God may have free course.' This is what he means here in Ephesians 6. 'Pray for me, that utterance may be given unto me, that I may open my mouth boldly, to make known the mystery of the gospel.'

And it still remains true after twenty centuries that there is only one effectual way for gospel work to be done. A man may speak with the tongues of men and of angels, but if there is not prayer behind his preaching it will just fall to the ground. And every preacher is entitled, as of right, to plead with his people and say, 'Pray for me, that utterance may be given me in the gospel.' Paul says in 2 Corinthians 4, 'If our gospel be hid, it is hid to them that are lost: in whom the god of this world hath blinded the minds of them which believe not, lest the light of the glorious gospel of Christ . . . shine unto them.' Well, that is the situation as it is. And Paul says that nothing but prayer can take the scales off their eyes. Prayer-saturated preaching! Saturate the preaching of the Word with the weapon of all-prayer, to mix the metaphors. Saturate it, and things will happen.

The weapon of all-prayer is the neglected piece of armour in the Christian armoury. Pray always; pray for all saints. Pray for me always, in the sense of a spirit of prayer—and that is a challenge as to what we are; it is what we are that matters. 'For all saints' —relating our battle to *the* battle, praying the battle forward and finding ourselves blessedly carried forward in the victory. And here is the focal point, the real thrust— 'for me, that utterance . . .' Paul does not mean eloquence; eloquence is a natural gift. There are some people very eloquent, and some not so eloquent; but that is not what matters, and we are far astray if we think what is needed is an eloquent voice in the pulpit. No, no, it is not eloquence; it is utterance. It is not even facility in getting the truth over; it is something indefinable. It is something like this: when the truth of God is being preached with utterance, it means that people who are listening are getting the message, and saying, 'Yes, that is it; I never saw that before. My word, that is startling.' That is utterance, and prayer is the only thing that can do it.